THE
TRANSFERENCE
OF
SPIRITS

Books By SAWO Media Publications

Samson Ajilore's Titles

Angels 101
The Revelation Of Paradise And Hell
Maturing In The Prophetic
Mercy Said No!
God, The Devil Or Just Me?
The School Of Seers
The Gifts Of The Holy Spirit
Activating & Developing The Prophet In You
The Lion And The Lamb
The Supernatural Power Of Unknown Tongues
Agapē Love, What It Really Means
How To Identify Your Gifts And Calling
How To Handle Sexual Feelings
How To Plead Your Case With God
How To Prophesy
Becoming A Healing Prophet
Angels And Demons
"Thus Says The Lord" In Relationships
Intimacy With The Holy Spirit
The Soul Winners
The Revealed Power Of Speaking In Tongues
The Transference Of Spirits
Secrets For Winning Marital Battles
Questions Women Ask
I Talk Back To The Devil
The Power Of Your Words

Fidelia Ajilore's Titles

Your Mouth And Your Destiny
Sisters In Waiting

THE TRANSFERENCE OF SPIRITS

By
SAMSON AJILORE

SAWO Media Publications 2016

Copyright ©2016 By Samson Ajilore
SAWO Media Publications SMP

Printed in USA.

All rights reserved. This book or any portion thereof may not be reproduced or used in any manner whatsoever without the express written permission of the publisher except for the use of brief quotations in a book review or scholarly journal.
All Scripture quotations unless otherwise indicated, are taken from the Holy Bible, NKJV-New King James Version. Other versions used include: King James Version (KJV), The Message Bible (MSG), Contemporary English Version (CEV), Weymouth's New Testament (WNT), New International Version (NIV), God's Word (GW) and World English Bible (WEB).

Second Edition: 2016

ISBN 978-1-329-76937-3

IN NIGERIA WRITE:
Samson Ajilore World Outreach SAWO
P. O. Box 957 Kubwa, Abuja, 901101
CALL: 08067419389
Email: agapevoice@live.com

IN THE U.S.A. WRITE:
Samson Ajilore World Outreach SAWO
435, Fawcett Ave #213 Tacoma, WA 98402
CALL: +1(253) 273-7933.
Email: sawousa@live.com
Visit: www.agapevoice.org

Dedicated to Bishop David Olaniyi Oyedepo. An unusual Apostle of faith from whom I'm priviledged to enjoy an indelible impartation of grace.

TABLE OF CONTENTS

PREFACE xi
1. THE TRANSFERENCE OF SPIRITS 1
   A.J. Gordon And E.W. Kenyon 4
   Poly And Smith Wigglesworth 6
   Smith Wigglesworth And Kenneth E. Hagin 8
   Kenneth E. Hagin And David Oyedepo 10
   Amiee Semple McPherson And Kathryn Khulman 12
   Kathryn Khulman And Benny Hinn 13
   Reinhard Bonnke And George Jeffreys 15
   William Branham And T.L. Osborn 17
2. THE ANOINTING WITHIN AND THE ONE UPON 21
   Summary 31
   Don't Write Yourself Off! 34
   Whoever Is Not Against Us Is For Us 36
   The Mantles Of Paul 38
   Perfect Gifts In Imperfect People 41
3. ELIJAH AND ELISHA 47
   Elijah's First Servant 49
   Elisha's Call 54
   Spiritually In Tune 59
   Offended Or Anointed? 62
   A Double Portion Will Not Come Cheaply 64
   The Anointing Is Not For Mockers 66
   Elisha And Gehazi 69
   Generational Mantles 72
   Entering Into The Mantles 76
   The Spirits Of Just Men Made Perfect 79
4. CAUTIONS! 83
   Lessons From Saul And Miriam 84
   Don't Duplicate An Error 87
   The Fast Food Syndrome! 90

- Mere Desire Is Not Enough 93
- Tarrying For The Glory 94
- War Against Religious Spirits 96
- Jesus Is Still The Same Today 98

5. THE LORD TAUGHT ME 101
- Sneaking Out Of School To Preach 103
- The Holy Spirit My Best Friend 105
- Our Helper In Prayer 108

6. HOW TO RECEIVE A PROPHET'S REWARD 111
- The Law Of Honour 113
- Prophets Do Not See Or Know Everything 122
- Testimonies Of Faith 125
- The Lingering Anointing 127
- The Dangerous Web Of Familiarity 130

ARE YOU REALLY SAVED? 135
- But I Go To Church 136
- But I'm A Preacher 136
- Salvation By Assumption 137
- Inherited Salvation? 138
- Bible Way To Be Saved 138
- An Advice For The Newly Saved 139

ABOUT THE AUTHOR 141
JOIN THE AGAPE PARTNERS 143
THREE LIFE CHANGING CLASSICS 152

Acknowledgement

My first gratitude goes to the precious Holy Spirit, my most intimate and greatly revered Friend and Helper of all times, for bringing me up in the supernatural from my childhood and teaching me how to really love, to worship and to pray.

To my affectionate wife, Fidelia Ajilore, a woman with an unusual passion for intercession. Thank you for standing by me in the work of ministry and making my little house into a beautiful home. You're such a darling!

To my adorable son, Samson Oluwanifemi Ajilore, you're a great blessing from God!

SAMSON AJILORE

PREFACE

When most people hear the expression "transference of spirits", the first thing that will probably cross their mind is transmitting of negative spirits or behaviours from one person to another by contact or association.

Even though the Bible clearly says that bad company corrupts good manners in 1Corinthians 15:33, it does not imply that every human character is a spirit which can be transmitted between two or more people.

Although, some negative characters have demonic spirits attached to them and thus, they can be transferred from one person to another. However, the believer is protected by the Holy Spirit and we are not to live in fear of unconscious demonic invasion.

The Bible speaks differently of the transference of spirits from the secular world. It speaks of the transference of the anointing of the Holy Spirit from one person to another person or people. This will result in the person or people to whom the spirit has been transferred, walking in similar or even greater manifestation of the Spirit than the person from whom it was transferred. We see this in Elisha, who did twice as much miracles as his spiritual father Elijah, after he received the mantle or transference of his twain spirit.

The Bible records that exactly twice as much miracles were done in the ministry of Elisha to that of Elijah. Elijah's last miracle (the parting of River Jordan) was Elisha's first. Consequently, he took off from where his spiritual father had stopped and advanced further beyond him.

The seventy elders had transference of spirit from Moses who was a prophet, and they began to prophesy like him immediately (Numbers 11:17-25).

King Saul found himself in the company of prophets and he began to prophesy so much that people started wondering if he had become one of the prophets (1Samuel 10:9-11). Joshua the son of Nun was full of the spirit of wisdom because Moses his spiritual father had laid hands upon him (Deuteronomy 34:9).

Elisha received a double portion of the spirit or anointing of his master or spiritual father, Elijah.

The transference of spirits didn't end in the Old Testament. In fact, the Old Testament closed with the promise of the messenger, whom God will send to prepare the way before the Messiah. That was John, who will come in the spirit and power of Elijah (Malachi 3:1; 4:5-6). There were 400 years of silence in which there was no other prophet since Malachi. And then, the New Testament kicks off with the fulfilment of Malachi's prophecy. John the Baptist or Baptizer came in the spirit and power of Elijah (Mark 1:1-6; Luke 1:11-17, 76; 7:27).

Even Jesus Himself confirmed it that he was the Elijah that was to come (Mathew 11:12-14; 17:12-13; Mark 9:12-13). John the Baptist was said to be the greatest of all prophets that had come before Jesus (Mathew 11:11). While all other prophets told the world that Jesus was coming, none of them personally introduced Him to the world like John had the priviledge of doing. He was the only prophet who saw Jesus in the flesh, baptized Him and revealed or publicized Him to the world. John looked towards Him and said, *"Behold the Lamb of God who takes away the sins of the world"* (John 1:29, 36).

Jesus also said that the list or smallest in the Kingdom of God is greater than John because he did not witness that Kingdom. John was an intertestamental prophet. He was beheaded shortly after Jesus began His public ministry (Mark 6). As such, he could not witness His death and resurrection which was the birthing of the Kingdom of God upon earth. Nobody could be born again until Jesus died and rose again and the Kingdom of God is made up of the Church, the born again or New Creation in Christ (2Corinthians 5:17-21).

To "transfer" means to convey something from one person to another. The word "spirit" as used in this book refers to the anointing of the Holy Spirit.

Read the second epistle of Peter and the book of Jude and you will see undeniable similarities between the two. Perhaps, Peter mentored Jude.

My spiritual Father E.J. El'Fransis is a prolific author and I do not struggle to write today. Something

THE TRANSFERENCE OF SPIRITS

of him is in me through association, submission and impartation.

Bishop David Oyedepo, the unusual Apostle of faith to whom this book is dedicated testifies on the transference of spirits. He said he received a supernatural transference of the spirit of boldness while listening to one of Reverend A.A. Allen's messages that was titled, "God is a killer!"

Papa, as we affectionately refer to him is a very humble but bold apostle of faith. He also makes reference to the impact that the ministry of Reverend Kenneth E. Hagin of blessed memory have on him. He even said that it was Hagin, whom he got connected to since 1976 that taught him the faith which set the stage for his life. And, from 1977, he connected with T. L. Osborn who taught him how to hear from God, without which he may not have been in the ministry today.

Bishop Oyedepo also testifies of the impartation of the spirit of wisdom that he received by the ministry of laying on of hands. It was through Pastor E. A. Adeboye, the humble General Overseer of the Redeemed Christian Church of God. I was priviledged to be counseled personally by Pastor Adeboye many years ago and my life and ministry has been transformed by that encounter. His voice is so full of Christ! His words sank deep into me... That man of God is so genuine!

I was under Bishop's ministration the first time he hosted Kenneth and Gloria Copeland. He pointed to Gloria in the face of over fifty thousand worshippers in the Faith Tabernacle and said, "This is the woman that taught me the mystery of prosperity!"

In another meeting, while teaching on mentorship Papa said, "If you see anyone with the kind of result that you desire, locate his step and walk in it and you will find yourself at the same level of result." He also declared that David Yonggi Cho mentored him in Church growth since 1985 and that it shows in the result he has in Church growth today. He is producing result after his order. He said, "Do you know that I've never sat with Paul Yonggi Cho in my life, yet he has been mentoring me since 1985?"

You can be mentored by someone through their resources or receive transference of spirit through books.

Isaac Newton once said, "If I have seen further, it is by standing on the shoulders of giants". If you wait to invent your own electricity before using light, you may die in darkness! Everybody is a product of more than one person. God wants to give you a new anointing if you're willing to humble yourself and receive.

Bishop Oyedepo said that he saw Hagin for the first time ten years after he has been following him through his resources. You don't have to wait until you can meet a person physically before connecting with the grace of God upon their life. Go for all their teachings and soak them in, praying for transference of grace until you draw the anointing by faith.

There is so much in life that one cannot accomplish alone and there are those who have already passed where you still aspire to be. Their wisdom can help you avoid a lot of mistakes or pitfalls and arrive faster at your destination in life. The transference of spirits is real!

I pray that the Lord by His precious Holy Spirit will open your understanding and minister to your heart as you study this insightful material. Prepare for the transference of spirits!

Love you so much, 1Corinthians 13
Samson Ajilore

SAMSON AJILORE

Chapter 1

THE TRANSFERENCE OF SPIRITS

"Remember those who rule over you, who have spoken the word of God to you, whose faith follow, considering the outcome of their conduct"
-Hebrews 13:7.

"He who receives you receives Me, and he who receives Me receives Him who sent Me. He who receives a prophet in the name of a prophet shall receive a prophet's reward. And he who receives a righteous man in the name of a righteous man shall receive a

righteous man's reward"
-Mathew 10:40-41.

This book is widely inspired by the teachings of Reverend Kenneth E. Hagin and Dr. David O. Oyedepo. I will like to begin by saying that no man is an island of himself. Everyone gets something from someone.

Jethro mentored Moses (Exodus 18). Something of Moses was upon Joshua his spiritual son (Deuteronomy 31; 3-8; 34; 9). Eli mentored Samuel (1Samuel 3). Samuel mentored Saul and David (1Samuel 9 and 16).

400 men, who were distressed, in debt and discontented with the way their life was going, gathered unto David in the Cave of Adullam. And, he mentored them unto greatness (1 Samuel 22).

David also mentored Solomon who mentored the Queen of Sheba and still continues to mentor countless today through his published works (1Kings 2:1-12; 10:1-13).

THE TRANSFERENCE OF SPIRITS

Something of Elijah was upon Elisha his spiritual son (1Kings 19; 19-21; 2Kings 2; 1-15) and Elisha mentored King Jehoash (2Kings 13:14).

Naomi mentored Ruth (Ruth 1-4). Mordecai mentored Esther (Esther 2:1-7).

Something of Jesus was upon the disciples (Acts 4:13), so visible that the people of Antioch nicknamed them "Christians" or followers of Christ (Acts 11:26).

Priscilla and Aquila mentored Apollos to become more effective and doctrinally accurate in ministry (Acts 18:24-28). Barnabas mentored Paul (Acts 9:26-30; 11:25-30). Something of Paul was upon Timothy his spiritual son (1 and 2 Timothy).

Paul the apostle believed in transference of spirits because he wrote; *"For I long to see you, that I may impart to you some spiritual gift, so that you may be established"* (Romans 1:11). Nobody is without a mentor. God mentored Adam in Eden and Adam mentored Eve (Genesis 1-3). God is the pioneer of mentorship and transference of spirits!

A.J. GORDON AND E.W. KENYON

Mentorship didn't end in the Bible. The popular grandfather of the modern "Word of Faith Movement", E.W. Kenyon of blessed memory rededicated his life to the Lord in A. J. Gordon's Church. Kenyon quoted from his books regularly in his writings. I can never forget the day I stumbled upon Gordon's books, "The ministry of the Holy Spirit" and "The Ministry of Healing" in our library during my fifth year in the Theological College. I read them over and again, alongside "The Gospel of Healing" by A. B. Simpson for a period of three months.

It became more vivid to me from that time first that healing was part of the finished work of Christ. And we are entitled to it just as we are to salvation from sin. And secondly, that the baptism with the Holy Spirit is equally for us today.

Faith begins where the will of God is known. I've seen countless receive healing and the baptism with the Holy Spirit under my ministry. But aside my calling from God, it was the understanding that I received through study that has imparted into me, the boldness to move in those things. I am so addicted to reading that my late mother walked up to me about 3:30 a.m. one day and said humorously, "You don't sleep in the morning, noon or at night, you're always reading...don't be surprised that you will start growing grey hairs very soon." She smiled and left.

I read most of Kenyon's 18 published works for the first time in Secondary School (High School). They're for the most part an exposition of the Pauline Epistles.

One of them even became my devotional for over five years. Some of their audio versions are part of my library today. I and my wife often let them play all through the night, alongside our audio Bibles. We sleep and wake up to the Word. What a great spiritual atmosphere!

I have drawn something from that man.

You see, words are spirits and it is the kind of words that prevail in a place that will determine the kind of spirits or atmosphere obtainable there.

POLY AND SMITH WIGGLESWORTH

I believe that Smith Wigglesworth was mentored by his wife Poly. Smith was an uneducated plumber who stuttered. His speech became fluent however when he received the baptism with the Holy Spirit. Initially, Poly was the one who used to do the preaching and let Smith make the altar call. But eventually, he grew cold. Nevertheless, she stood in gap for him, in love and character. Until he was back on his feet and became the apostle of faith that history later recorded.

How we need women like that today! It was also a woman who ministered the baptism with the Holy Spirit to Smith; *"But you shall receive power when the Holy Spirit has come upon you; and you shall be witnesses to Me in Jerusalem, and in all Judea and Samaria, and to the end of the earth"* (Acts 1:8). Smith said that he owes all he is, in his entire ministry to Poly. Smith's only available video is that of him taking Poly on a walk. They were both holding hands and he was kissing her on the walkway. He was a good husband, not just a man of miracles; *"Husbands, love your wives, just as Christ also loved the Church and gave Himself for her that He might sanctify and cleanse her with the washing of water by the word"* (Ephesians 5:25-26).

I could remember how I travelled to Kaduna for the first time, several years back. It was to look for "SMITH WIGGLESWORTH, the Complete collections of his life teachings" and also those of John G. Lake and Maria Etter. Great books compiled by Roberts Liardon. I had to sell an expensive wrist watch that someone had presented to me. I added it up with the money that my parents gave me for Christmas clothes and shoe that year to make the journey and get those books.

The spiritual is more important than the material in every respect. Faith leaps upon me from the pages of those books! The spirits of those men lingers upon their literatures!

Among other things, Smith taught me that fear looks but faith jumps and Lake that electricity is God's power in the physical the same way the anointing is His power in the spiritual. The spiritual governs the natural. It is our spiritual inputs that will determine our physical exploits. One who feeds his spirit well will have enough strength to sustain his weaknesses.

SMITH WIGGLESWORTH AND KENNETH E. HAGIN

Something of Wigglesworth and E.W. Kenyon robbed off on Kenneth E. Hagin. Hagin was an unusual prophet of God.

Hagin never met Smith. He didn't know the man personally. However, he read about him constantly, actually wearing his books out, until something from Smith rubbed off on him.

Hagin's hundreds of video, audio and books have contributed immensely to my spiritual advancements in life and ministry. I learnt from his Memorial Service video that before praying for the sick, he would always take his watch off and lay it on the podium. This is because the anointing will stop his watches from working.

Sometimes, the anointing would also settle upon Hagin's legs so much, until he couldn't move them. He had men who were constantly behind him as he ministers. So that they could hold him up when the anointing becomes too strong that he cannot stand. That prophet of God was so anointed!

THE TRANSFERENCE OF SPIRITS

Hagin even prophesied of his own departure from earth. His son, Kenneth Hagin Junior acknowledged during the Memorial Service that Dad Hagin had prophesied concerning 2003 being a year of preparation and separation. He said there will be tears (weeping) and grief shall be endured but joy comes in the morning. He went to be with the Lord in September of that same year. His last moments and conversations with his family revealed that he was ready for home and unwilling to stay back any longer.

I was not privileged to meet with Hagin physically but I followed his ministry closely through his books, audios and videos. I still do till today. One time, he appeared to me in a vision and gave me a golden pen, after laying his hands upon me as I was cooking on a stove. I know that something of that great man of God is upon my life and ministry today, especially on my writings.

God can bring us into a deeper dimension of the anointing through the ministry of others who have gone ahead of us. *"Remember your leaders, who spoke the word of God to you. Consider the outcome of their way of life and imitate their faith"* (Hebrews 13:7 NIV).

KENNETH E. HAGIN AND DAVID OYEDEPO

Something of Hagin is evident upon David Oyedepo, the presiding Bishop of the Living Faith Church, also known as Winner's Chapel. Even the chairs in the Church's International Headquaters known as Faith Tabernacle, in Ota, Nigeria are products of the gift of faith. And, that faith is the invisible pillar of that great building.

Bishop Oyedepo's teachings are what I can only describe as those of an unusual apostle sent from God. He preaches faith after the order of Hagin! I've read numerous of his books and listened to countless of his tapes over and again, until something of him evidently robbed off on me.

Living Faith Church is our family Church. My parents served at the Kaduna Headquarters in Barnawa, during the late 90s until they moved to Abuja where they both continued to serve faithfully, at the Kubwa branch.

Dad is in the Sanctuary Keeper Unit where I also served at one time. My late mother worked with the Protocol and Hospitality Unit until she graduated to be with the Lord in October 2014. She even told me of how she used to attend Bishop's meetings in Ilorin, during the 80s.

I was priviledged to undergo the Word of Faith Bible Institute (WOFBI) and also got married at Living Faith Church.

I've encountered Bishop Oyedepo severally in my visions...One time, he looked into my eyes and rays of light flashed upon me until my eyes became radiant like his...I was imparted with a new anointing! The next time I stood to preach, people said that my voice and passion were like his.

This generation is blessed to have such a great man of God. He's purely unusual!

It is rather unfortunate that many today do not accept most of the prophets that God sends to them. We don't have to wait till people die before testifying of how their ministry has imparted our life. God is not confined to the past. He didn't die in history. He is still working in our midst today and it is our duty to recognize and honour those He has raised among us.

AMIEE SEMPLE MCPHERSON AND KATHRYN KHULMAN

In "God's Generals", a 12-volume biographical video series, Roberts Liardon tells how Aimee received transference of spirit. As a young would-be evangelist, she went to visit Mother Maria Etter. Etter was in her golden years and she passed on her mantle to young Aimee. Liardon goes on to explain how her mantle then passed onto Kathryn Kuhlman, and then onto Benny Hinn of our time. God is a generational God!

Maria Etter's books, "Holy Ghost Sermons" and "Signs and Wonders" are for me, books of a thousand blessings!

When Kathryn Khulman, the great apostle of the Holy Spirit was young, she said that she would be the next Amiee Semple McPherson. Amiee's book, "This is that" is life changing!

Amiee was a woman of miracles and the founder of the Church of the Foursquare Gospel whose ministry Kathryn had followed very closely.

KATHRYN KHULMAN AND BENNY HINN

Something of Kathryn Khulman is evident upon Benny Hinn, the world renowned healing evangelist. In fact, someone has called him the "male fashion" of Kathryn.

I can't express how I feel each time I read Kathryn and Benny's books and watch their Miracle Service videos. Willis "Doc" Horton, who taught at Rhema for 13 years, spoke in Kenneth E. Hagin's Memorial Service's video. He shared how powerfully Kathryn Kuhlman ministered together with Kenneth E. Hagin at New York City. It was during a meeting he was priviledged to have attended in the 60s. Doc sat between the two of them and his life never remained the same again. Imagine sitting between such generals!

The First time I read "Good Morning Holy Spirit" by Benny, I wept like a baby from the first page till the last. It imparted into me a deeper spiritual hunger. I was still in High School. It was that book that led me to go searching for Kathryn's materials. I went after all that was available of her.

I searched different bookshops across the country, the internet, and even made advanced payments to people for her materials.

I saw beyond the white flowing gowns of Kathryn or the white beautiful suits of Benny. I looked beyond, until I began to see them transfigured. I even enrolled for ministry tutelage under Benny Hinn, at his Signs and Wonders School of Ministry. It's life transforming.

Those who are not spiritually inclined will criticize everything. They have so much to say against Benny Hinn's visit to Kathryn Khulman's grave. He followed her in life and death! If the anointing could linger on the decaying bones of an Old Testament Elisha, why can't it on a New Testament Kathryn?

I can't tell you what I saw by the Spirit when I was priviledged in the company of an old prophet to visit where the late Apostle Joseph Ayo Babalola of the Christ Apostolic Church (C.A.C) was buried. The anointing on departed saints never dies!

REINHARD BONNKE AND GEORGE JEFFREYS

I remember what Evangelist Reinhard Bonnke told us at a minister's Fire Conference many years ago. He shared his testimony about how he stumbled at the house of famous Evangelist, George Jeffreys in UK.

He knocked on the door and a certain woman answered it. He asked if the house belonged to the famous George Jeffreys, who shook England in the 1940's and she said yes. He went on to ask, "Is he alive?" She said "Yes." Then conversation went on until he asked if he could see him. And the woman was quick to say "No."

He felt so disappointed but then, he heard a deep voice coming from the inside.

It said, "Let him come in".

When he walked in, he saw a frail old man and after some introductions, Evangelist Jeffreys laid his hand upon Bonnke and blessed him.

Bonnke said, "I staggered out of the door because the presence of God was all over him". God's power doesn't fade with age. When he arrived back in Germany, he received the news about George Jeffreys' death from his father.

I don't think that Africa has seen a greater Evangelist than Reinhard Bonnke. He is possibly the greatest evangelist that we have seen in our generation. Yet, he was not self-made; he got the mantle from someone.

Every story of greatness is traceable to an input from someone else or other people.

Pride and arrogance has kept so many back from walking in greater anointing. God promised to fill the hungry. Once you're contented with your present state, you cannot have more.

There must be a holy desperation in your heart for more of God. You must be willing to forget yesterday and reach for a deeper realm. God cannot be exhausted. There is still so much with Him reserved for you.

WILLIAM BRANHAM AND T.L. OSBORN

T.L. Osborn was a great missionary to India. He gave his testimony in a video interview on Trinity Broadcasting Network (TBN) one time. He said that he heard a thousand voices calling him to the ministry of signs and wonders while listening to William Branham, who was an unusual healing prophet.

I've watched several of Branham and Osborn's miracle videos and listened to their more than a few audios. There is an undeniable anointing of God's Spirit upon those men. However, some people have raised concern about certain doctrines of Branham. Just as they have of John Dowie, another great healing apostle. Nevertheless, the truth is that, only a fool will doubt that God's anointing was upon those men. When I was in the Theological College, I was taught how to separate the edible from the poisonous.

God's servants are not perfect but they carry some perfect anointing.

We can aim for those anointing without duplicating or criticizing their imperfections. We can follow after Abraham without birthing Ishmael in the flesh; *"Listen to Me, you who follow after righteousness, You who seek the LORD: Look to the rock from which you were hewn, And to the hole of the pit from which you were dug. Look to Abraham your father, And to Sarah who bore you; For I called him alone, And blessed him and increased him"* (Isaiah 51:1-2).

Anyone pursuing the anointing on other people's life must endeavour to maintain a balance in the Scriptures. Otherwise, he might wind up in errors. Anointed people are not infallible, only the Bible is.

I learn from other people but there is nobody that I read more than my Bible. And, I don't listen to anyone more than I do to the Holy Spirit. Don't let any voice replace the Holy Spirit in your life and never allow any book to replace the Bible.

I cannot say how many books of Benny and Kathryn I have read and how many times. Everybody in my house got to know about them from me.

If you love the anointing, you will love the anointed and hold them preciously together with all

THE TRANSFERENCE OF SPIRITS

that proceeds from them. Whatever comes from the anointed carries the anointing!

Nobody has taught me more about the Holy Spirit and His anointing than Kathryn and Benny apart from the Bible. I read, watched and listened to those two generals of faith until I started having visions of them. My favourite of all Kathryn's books is "The Greatest Power in the World." The Holy Spirit's anointing is the greatest power in the world!

I can't continue to relate one after the other, all the experiences and supernatural encounters that I have had from reading, listening and watching video teachings by anointed men and women of God.

You can learn more about Smith Wigglesworth, Kathryn Kuhlman, Amie McPherson and several others in Roberts Liadorn's biographical video and book series titled, "God's Generals".

SAMSON AJILORE

Chapter 2

THE ANOINTING WITHIN AND THE ONE UPON

There are two major streams of the anointing that works in the life of a believer. One is the anointing within and the other is the one upon.

The Holy Spirit within us is a divine Personality but His anointing upon us is His power. We relate and commune with the Person, but we use the anointing or power.

It is not the Holy Spirit that we command here and there when we minister to people. He is also not the One that we put inside the handkerchiefs and bottles of water or oil but the anointing that we have from Him that is resting upon us.

God anointed Jesus with the Holy Spirit (a Person) within and power (His anointing) upon. The anointing upon is power for ministry; *"THE SPIRIT OF THE LORD IS UPON ME, Because He has anointed Me To preach the gospel to the poor; He has sent Me to heal the brokenhearted, To proclaim liberty to the captives And recovery of sight to the blind, To set at liberty those who are oppressed"* (Luke 4:18).

The Holy Spirit within Jesus was the secret to a life of sacrifice and a deep relationship with God. It was through that indwelling Spirit or anointing within that He offered Himself to God spotless; *"How much more shall the blood of Christ, WHO THROUGH THE ETERNAL SPIRIT OFFERED HIMSELF WITHOUT SPOT TO GOD, cleanse your conscience from dead works to serve the living God?"* (Hebrews 9:14). It was the anointing within that sustained Jesus, not the one upon.

THE TRANSFERENCE OF SPIRITS

Jesus communed with the Holy Spirit (God's Presence or Person) that is within Him. And then, He used His power (anointing) that was upon Him to do good and heal all that were oppressed of the devil; *"How God anointed Jesus of Nazareth with THE HOLY SPIRIT AND WITH POWER, who went about doing good and healing all who were oppressed by the devil, for God was with Him"* (Acts 10:38).

It wasn't the Holy Spirit that left Jesus and went out to heal the woman with the issue of blood, it was the anointing upon Him; *"But Jesus said, "Somebody touched Me, for I PERCEIVED POWER GOING OUT FROM ME"* (Luke 8:46).

The Holy Spirit that was within Jesus never left Him during His earthly ministry. On the other hand, His power upon Him did a thousand times and over; *"And the whole multitude sought to touch Him, for POWER WENT OUT FROM HIM AND HEALED THEM ALL"* (Luke 6:19).

The sick folks of Jesus' days didn't only follow Him to hear a good sermon. They knew their healing was sure because of the anointing upon Him. They came both to hear and to be healed, since faith comes by hearing; *"And he came down with them, and stood in the plain, and the company of his disciples, and a great multitude of people out of all Judaea and Jerusalem, and from the sea coast of Tyre and Sidon, WHICH CAME TO HEAR HIM, AND TO BE HEALED OF THEIR DISEASES"* (Luke 6:17).

We cannot transfer or impart the anointing within who is the indwelling person and presence of the Holy Spirit. Nevertheless, we can transfer and impart the anointing upon us which is God's power for service or ministry.

We can have a replenishment or fresh anointing come upon us but we cannot have another refill or top-up of the anointing within.

The power upon us can increase, the Person within us cannot.

We all have the same Holy Spirit within us, not that some have His hands and others His legs. It is the anointing or power upon us that is given in measures (John 3:34).

SPIRIT, SOUL AND BODY

The Scripture distinguishes between the spirit, soul and body. It doesn't portray them all as one but as three separate parts. Now, let us study the three of them in relation to the anointing within and the one upon;

1THESSALONIANS 5:23
23 Now may the God of peace Himself sanctify you completely; and may your whole SPIRIT, SOUL, and BODY be preserved blameless at the coming of our Lord Jesus Christ.

You're a spirit: The spirit is the real you. It sustains your weaknesses (Proverbs 18:14). It is God's lamp to your other parts (Proverbs 20:27). With your spirit, you relate with God in the spirit realm (John 4:24). <u>The anointing WITHIN is permanently in your spirit (1John 2:20; 2:27).</u>

You have a soul: Your soul is made up of your will (power to choose), thoughts and feelings or emotions of all sorts. It is your contact with the mental or intellectual realm (Genesis 2:7). It can get tied to someone and fall in love or lust depending on where you channel it (Genesis 34:3-8; 1Samuel 18:1).

It departs from the body alongside the spirit when the body dies (Genesis 35:18; Ecclesiastes 3:21). <u>The anointing UPON rests upon your soul and body and influences them (Acts 1:8; 2-3).</u>

You live in a physical body: The body is the physical house or tent that you live in. It is your contact with the physical realm. <u>The anointing UPON rests on your body and soul (Acts 1:8; 2-3).</u>

The anointing upon (God's power) does not leave your body even after death. Remember that it remained upon Elisha's bones long after his physical death (2Kings 13:21). It is the lingering anointing.

You're a spirit who has a soul and lives in a physical body.

At creation, your spirit, soul and body were fully in harmony with God. You had full spiritual life. During the fall, you died spiritually. The three were affected. They were separated from God, disconnected from spiritual life and became joined to the nature of the devil (Genesis 3; Ephesians 2:3). Spiritual death is not cessation of life but another form of life. It means to be dead to God but alive to the devil and his evil nature.

At the new birth, your spirit was regenerated, it was created anew like a new born baby; *"Therefore, if anyone is in Christ, he is a new creation; old things have passed away; behold, all things have become new"* (2Corinthians 5:17). The Holy Spirit (the anointing within) mingled with your spirit at salvation and the two of you became one and inseparable.

It is like pouring one glass of water in another glass that contains water, you cannot separate the waters anymore. You became joined to the Lord as one spirit; *"But he who is joined to the Lord is one spirit with Him"* (1Corinthians 6:17). That is the moment that the anointing within becomes yours. It is God giving you Himself in the Person of the Holy Spirit to indwell you forever (John 14:16; 1John 2:20: 2:27).

That anointing within abides in you so that you will abide in Him; *"But the anointing which you have received from Him ABIDES IN YOU, and you do not need that anyone teach you; but as the same anointing teaches you concerning all things, and is true, and is not a lie, and just as it has taught you, YOU WILL ABIDE IN HIM"* (1John 2:27). The Spirit within doesn't come and go or diminishes and increases like the anointing that comes upon you.

The indwelling Spirit of God is not a temporal lease based on terms and conditions. He is an eternal gift of God based on faith in the finished work of Christ. It is this indwelling Spirit that produces spiritual hunger within you. So as a spiritual new born baby, you start desiring the sincere milk of the Word of God, in order to grow (1Peter 2:2). The first thing that happens to a new born baby immediately after birth is hunger for breastmilk. That's what happens to you the moment you're saved.

The inward anointing also begins to witness with your spirit that you're God's child (Romans 8:16). That's divine assurance. You receive the indwelling presence and Person of the Holy Spirit and you cannot be separated from Him any longer. On the other hand, your soul and body are still as old. Only that they are now being influenced by the indwelling Holy Spirit in your regenerated spirit. That is why the Bible talks of submitting your body to the Lord and renewing your mind with the Word so that they can also be aligned with God like the spirit;

ROMANS 12:1-2
1 I beseech you therefore, brethren, by the mercies of God, that you PRESENT YOUR BODIES A LIVING SACRIFICE, HOLY, ACCEPTABLE TO GOD, which is your reasonable service.
2 And do not be conformed to this world, but BE TRANSFORMED BY THE RENEWING OF YOUR MIND, that you may prove what is that good and acceptable and perfect will of God.

You receive the anointing upon as God's power on your soul and body at the moment you're baptized with the Holy Spirit (Acts 1:8). This anointing is given for Christian service or ministry. The soul is also called the mind. It is the Word of God that renews the soul. The Psalmist says in the 23rd Psalm, *"He makes me to lie down in green pastures; He leads me beside the still waters. He restores my soul; He leads me in the paths of righteousness For His name's sake."*

It is very dangerous to abandon the renewal of the soul. Many who have done so are now using the anointing upon them for personal profit. They've corrupted it. If you do not renew your soul with the Word of God constantly, it might end up siding with the devil. I've seen a lot of anointed people of God who have failed to use the anointing within to keep the one upon.

The anointing upon does not produce character; it only produces miracle, signs and wonders. It is the anointing within that produces character in union with the born again human spirit (Galatians 5:22). Without yielding to the anointing within, we can easily corrupt the one upon. Paul the apostle wrote to Timothy the young minister concerning this truth; *"Guard the good deposit that was entrusted to you--guard it with the help of the Holy Spirit who lives in us"* (1Timothy 1:14 NIV).

We must protect the anointing upon us by the Holy Spirit within us. Many have allowed the manipulative spirit of Jezebel to highjack and corrupt the anointing upon them. They have failed to protect that anointing by yielding to the indwelling Spirit and walking closely with the Lord. They have become spiritual charlatans, peddling the unction of God for self-gain.

THE TRANSFERENCE OF SPIRITS

SUMMARY

Having a personal walk with the Lord is more important than having the anointing upon you. The Holy Spirit is the anointing within, His power is the anointing upon you.

The anointing within is indwelling. It is always there. It never diminishes. It never increases. That anointing is a Person. The Holy Spirit Himself. It is not as if some have the head of the Holy Spirit only while others have His full body.

The Person of the Holy Spirit is equally present in every believer but His power upon them is in measures.

The anointing upon is supernatural ability, influence, or might of the Spirit and it comes for a reason and stays for a season. It can be more or less. It can be stronger at some time than other times. It is not always there like the one within.

The anointing within is the presence and person of God. The one upon is the power or ability of God. You cannot have more of God but you can have more of His anointing, ability or power. Every believer has the same anointing WITHIN but some are more or less anointed UPON.

When the Bible speaks of Jesus having the Spirit without measure, it doesn't refer to the Spirit within but the One upon (John 3:34). The Spirit within have no measure but the one upon can be more or less.

It is the anointing within that preserves the one upon, not the other way round. People are always seeking the power but they don't know the danger of not understanding what they're asking for. It is a heavy responsibility.

God's power is a mighty tool for service and not a childish toy to showcase self.

The anointing within is contrasted against the one upon in the next table:

THE TRANSFERENCE OF SPIRITS

	The Holy Spirit/Anointing UPON (Acts 1:8)	The Holy Spirit/Anointing WITHIN (1John 2:27)
1	God's power for ministry	God Himself in the person of the Holy Spirit
2	Comes at Holy Spirit's baptism for ministry	Comes at salvation for relationship
3	Can increase or reduce	Can't increase or reduce
4	Produces spiritual gifts or anointing	Produces spiritual fruit or character
5	Comes for a reason and stays for a season	Always abiding and never leaves
6	Comes upon your body and soul	Always abiding within your spirit
7	Can be corrupted	Cannot be corrupted
8	Cannot protect you from deception (Remember Balaam, Samson & Judas)	Protects you from deception
9	Cannot protect the anointing within	Can protect the anointing upon
10	Doesn't guarantee eternity with God	Guarantees eternity with God
11	Largely depends upon people and atmosphere (Remember Jesus' experience in Mark 6)	Doesn't depend on people and atmosphere but on relationship with God

DON'T WRITE YOURSELF OFF!

God doesn't really have any problem with weak or flawed people. This was why He could use folks like:

1. Noah the drunk who cursed his son
2. Abram the old man who slept with Hagar
3. Jacob who was a trickster
4. Moses the murderer who stammered
5. David the adulterer and murderer
6. Rahab the prostitute
7. Miriam the gossip
8. Samson who was weak with women
9. Gideon who was afraid and insecure
10. Elijah who roasted people with his anointing
11. Jeremiah who was too young
12. Jonah the runaway prophet without mercy
13. Peter who denied Him thrice
14. Thomas who doubted Him
15. Judas who was a thief and also sold Him out
16. Mary the Magdalene who had seven demons
17. Paul the serial killer who also had a thorn
18. He even used dead Lazarus!

1CORINTHIANS 1:26-29
26 For you see your calling, brethren, that not many wise according to the flesh, not many mighty, not many noble, are called.
27 BUT GOD HAS CHOSEN THE FOOLISH THINGS OF THE WORLD TO PUT TO SHAME THE WISE, AND GOD HAS CHOSEN THE WEAK THINGS OF THE WORLD TO PUT TO SHAME THE THINGS WHICH ARE MIGHTY;
28 AND THE BASE THINGS OF THE WORLD AND THE THINGS WHICH ARE DESPISED GOD HAS CHOSEN, and the things which are not, to bring to nothing the things that are,
29 that no flesh should glory in His presence.

God doesn't use super humans because there are no super humans. He picks up the filthy, messy, broken, abused, battered, shattered, dirty and drunk and so on and so forth and qualifies them despite their flaws because of His unconditional love. There are no super men and women of God, just ordinary flawed people who encountered His extraordinary grace and began to do the extraordinary.

My life and ministry has been greatly blessed by the impartations of several giants of faith. Most of them, I know not in the flesh but in the Spirit. We don't have to be discouraged by our inability to meet many of these generals of faith in person. Faith can connect from anywhere. There is no such thing as time and distance in the realm of the spirit. We can connect that realm through faith and the Holy Spirit because, we are born of the Spirit and are spirits; *"That which is born of the flesh is flesh, and that which is born of the Spirit is spirit"* (John 3:6).

WHOEVER IS NOT AGAINST US IS FOR US

There was a certain man that was casting out devils in the name of Jesus but the disciples asked him to stop because he didn't follow them. Those men saw themselves as the "people of the Saviour", "the inner circle", and "the new guys in town". They obviously had a lot on their minds about others outside their circle.

John was happy to report to the Lord that they had just stopped an "impostor" who was not part of the "circles" of the "Jesus movement" but Jesus rebuked them.

THE TRANSFERENCE OF SPIRITS

There is a very important lesson in this story. Especially because all sorts of divisions are on in the Church on who takes the mantle of whom. And, who is the true disciple and has the right to the mantle of whom. Jesus rebuked the disciples for forbidding that man and told them that whoever was not against them was for them (Luke 9:49-50).

It is really funny that there are many close disciples today who have not really caught the fire and the truth that several distant disciples have caught. The connectivity with the grace of God is not just a matter of physical contact but of genuine spiritual connection.

The spirit of the prophets resides in their words, either spoken or written. Consequently, we can school ourselves in their Holy Spirit's inspired teachings in video, audio, or written formats available.

God will never mock a hungry heart. In fact, He has promised that those who hunger and thirst spiritually will be filled (Mathew 5:6; John 7:37-38).

THE MANTLES OF PAUL

ACTS 19:1-12

1 ¶ And it happened, while Apollos was at Corinth, that Paul, having passed through the upper regions, came to Ephesus. And finding some disciples

2 he said to them, "Did you receive the Holy Spirit when you believed?" So they said to him, "We have not so much as heard whether there is a Holy Spirit."

3 And he said to them, "Into what then were you baptized?" So they said, "Into John's baptism."

4 Then Paul said, "John indeed baptized with a baptism of repentance, saying to the people that they should believe on Him who would come after him, that is, on Christ Jesus."

5 When they heard this, they were baptized in the name of the Lord Jesus.

6 And when Paul had laid hands on them, the Holy Spirit came upon them, and they spoke with tongues and prophesied.

7 Now the men were about twelve in all.

8 ¶ And he went into the synagogue and spoke boldly for three months, reasoning and persuading concerning the things of the kingdom of God.

9 But when some were hardened and did not believe, but spoke evil of the Way before the multitude, he departed from them and withdrew the disciples, reasoning daily in the school of Tyrannus.

**10 And this continued for two years, so that all who dwelt in Asia heard the word of the Lord Jesus, both Jews and Greeks.
11 NOW GOD WORKED UNUSUAL MIRACLES BY THE HANDS OF PAUL,
12 SO THAT EVEN HANDKERCHIEFS OR APRONS WERE BROUGHT FROM HIS BODY TO THE SICK, AND THE DISEASES LEFT THEM AND THE EVIL SPIRITS WENT OUT OF THEM.**

The mantles of Paul carried the tangible supernatural anointing that was upon his life and ministry and humans are more than handkerchiefs. You can carry the same anointing and even greater by faith.

One of the earliest miracles in my ministry was the sudden disappearance of a swollen in the scrotum from a sixteen year old boy, who was born with that abnormality. I was only a teenager at the time. The miracle took place as I ministered, after reading "Releasing The Supernatural", a great book by Bishop David Oyedepo. Something of that unusual man of God is in me!

God has ordained that people should be channels of blessings to others upon earth.

There are men and women in the Church of Jesus Christ from generation to generation who have the grace of God upon their lives for the transformation of lives and the Kingdom advancements.

Our God is a generational God, who wants their mantles to be passed on to other generations. But oftentimes, we cannot enter into these mantles because we evaluate their shortcomings rather than appreciate the grace of God upon them.

The Scripture says for us to follow their faith, not their character flaws.

From Genesis to Revelation, there are life accounts of people of great exploits of faith, but also with various weaknesses. The only exception is Jesus Christ, the same yesterday, today and forever. God can use anybody.

PERFECT GIFTS IN IMPERFECT PEOPLE

Christ is the only perfect One. All others are still in the process of perfection.

The reason for His distribution of gifts in the Church is for our perfection or maturity;

EPHESIANS 4:11-16
11 And He Himself gave some to be apostles, some prophets, some evangelists, and some pastors and teachers,
12 for the equipping of the saints for the work of ministry, for the edifying of the body of Christ,
13 TILL WE ALL COME TO THE UNITY OF THE FAITH AND OF THE KNOWLEDGE OF THE SON OF GOD, TO A PERFECT MAN, TO THE MEASURE OF THE STATURE OF THE FULLNESS OF CHRIST;
14 THAT WE SHOULD NO LONGER BE CHILDREN, TOSSED TO AND FRO AND CARRIED ABOUT WITH EVERY WIND OF DOCTRINE, BY THE TRICKERY OF MEN, IN THE CUNNING CRAFTINESS OF DECEITFUL PLOTTING,
15 BUT, SPEAKING THE TRUTH IN LOVE, MAY GROW UP IN ALL THINGS INTO HIM WHO IS THE HEAD-- CHRIST--
16 from whom the whole body, joined and knit together by what every joint supplies, according to the

effective working by which every part does its share, causes growth of the body for the edifying of itself in love.

Even in the midst of Eli's imperfections, God still refused to jump over to Samuel, so He spoke to him in the voice of Eli (1 Samuel 3).

God also didn't take it easy with Miriam and Aaron for speaking against His servant Moses over making the choice of an Ethiopian wife.

We just have to understand with God that His vessels may not be perfect but His gifts are. So let's get the gifts and leave the weakness "part" to the God whose strength is made perfect in our weaknesses (2Corinthians 12:9). *"Who are you to judge another's servant? To his own master he stands or falls. Indeed, he will be made to stand, for God is able to make him stand"* (Romans 14:4).

God has chosen to use the weak and foolish people like me and you so that no flesh will boast in His presence (1Corinthians 1:27). And, if you think that God is pretty impressed at your own great strength, keep it up.

Perfection is cultivated but gifts are perfectly given, so there will always be perfect gifts in imperfect people.

We should follow the character of Christ alone. Nevertheless, we can imitate the faith of those who have broken through in certain areas of life by faith. We should follow their faith, considering the end of their conversation, so that we can start where they stop and do greater works.

It is important to know that only the one that receives a prophet in the name of a prophet will get a prophet's reward.

Therefore, the question is this; in whose name do we receive the prophet that God sends to us? This question is important especially in these days when everyone is a brother. Do we receive our prophets in the name of a friend, teacher, brother, righteous person or a prophet? The answer determines the reward.

A righteous person has his own reward and so also does a prophet but Jesus did not mix or advice that we mix the two together;

MATHEW 10:41
40 "He who receives you receives Me, and he who receives Me receives Him who sent Me.
41 "HE WHO RECEIVES A PROPHET IN THE NAME OF A PROPHET SHALL RECEIVE A PROPHET'S REWARD. AND HE WHO RECEIVES A RIGHTEOUS MAN IN THE NAME OF A RIGHTEOUS MAN SHALL RECEIVE A RIGHTEOUS MAN'S REWARD.
42 "And whoever gives one of these little ones only a cup of cold water in the name of a disciple, assuredly, I say to you, he shall by no means lose his reward."

Genuine heart to heart connection and honour is required for true transference of spirit. Disloyalty and dishonour will disqualify from impartation;

PROVERBS 27:18-19
18 Whoever keeps the fig tree will eat its fruit; So he who waits on his master will be honoured.
19 As in water face reflects face, So a man's heart reveals the man.

THE TRANSFERENCE OF SPIRITS

I understand as a poet that one of the best ways to become a great poet is by reading classical poets. Everybody gets something from someone.

One of the reasons why revival tarries is that we would not celebrate and honour the fathers and mothers in the Church; *"Let the elders that rule well be counted worthy of double honour, especially they who labour in the word and doctrine"* (1 Timothy 5:17).

This is one of the reasons the Lord God has sent the spirit of Elijah to turn the heart of the fathers to the children, and the heart of the children to their fathers. And, the disobedient to the wisdom of the just. To make ready a people prepared for the Lord; *"He will also go before Him in the spirit and power of Elijah, 'to turn the hearts of the fathers to the children,' and the disobedient to the wisdom of the just, to make ready a people prepared for the Lord"* (Luke 1:17).

Honour and unpretentious spiritual heart to heart connectivity is a must requirement for genuine impartation.

CHAPTER 3

ELIJAH AND ELISHA

The first time the Bible mentions Elijah, it was during the reign of King Ahab the son of Omri. He became king in the 38th year of Asa the king of Judah and reigned over Israel in Samaria for 22 years. Ahab married Jezebel a princess. She was the daughter of Ethbaal, king of the Sidonians. And so, Ahab abandoned Jehovah. He served Baal and worshipped Asherah instead, because of Jezebel's influence. He even set up an altar for Baal and provoked God with his wickedness and idolatry (1 Kings 16:29-34).

Now in the midst of all these evil, Elijah who was briefly introduced as the Tishbite shows up with a word from the Lord. He confronted Ahab with a prophecy of drought as judgement from the Lord.

During that drought, Elijah was away. God sustained him supernaturally and even used him to sustain a starving widow in Zarephath and revived her dead son (1Kings 17).

After three years of drought and severe famine in Samaria, God told Elijah to confront King Ahab again with the prophecy of rain. Obadiah, a God fearing chief servant of Ahab has been hiding God's true prophets from Jezebel's sword. He bumps into Elijah.

Elijah challenged and defeated 850 prophets of Baal and Asherah. He killed all of them by the Brook of Kishon to the shame of Jezebel who has been executing God's true prophets. He restored the reverence and worship of Jehovah back to the Land (1Kings 18:1-40).

Now, after the defeat of the false prophets, Elijah told Ahab to go and feast because the rain is coming. Elijah on the other hand went up to the top of Mount Carmel to travail in prayers for the rain he had prophesied (1Kings 18:41-42; James 5:17-18).

ELIJAH'S FIRST SERVANT

You see, for the first time, we read of Elijah's servant in 1 Kings 18:43. The unnamed servant was not Elisha. He could have been the one that receives the double portion anointing. But, he doesn't strike me like someone who knows how to stick close like Elisha.

His first recorded mission was to go and look at a certain direction until he sees something. But he kept returning hurriedly to his master with no positive report. He wasn't patient and enduring. Elijah had to send him back seven times to go and look again until he finally saw the sign of rain.

Imagine what kind of an apprentice that you have to instruct seven times repeatedly over a single task.

The second task was for him to go and tell Ahab to go down before the rain stops him (1 Kings 18: 44-46). Elijah also left Mount Carmel and it rained heavily. His servant definitely left with him

When Ahab got home, he reported everything to Jezebel that Elijah had done. She was angry that her false prophets were killed.

Jezebel sent words to Elijah that may the gods kill her if she fails to kill him in 24 hours. Elijah ran in fear and fled to Beersheba, a place that belongs to Judah. Now, that was the second and the last time his unnamed servant was mentioned. This time there was no task. We simply read in 1Kings 19:3 that Elijah left his servant in Beersheba.

This servant was nothing like Elisha the determined warrior. We know that Elijah had the attitude of leaving his servant behind but Elisha never consented to that.

The unnamed servant witnessed great miracles wrought by Elijah. He saw the Lord working through him mightily and was definitely glad to be associated with such a prophet. He was with him as long as the going was smooth. I believe he enjoyed the prophet offerings, the gifts and the priviledge of being the one that people will go through to see his master. However, he left Elijah to walk alone in the wilderness of trial when his ministry came under heavy witchcraft attack and death threat.

There are so many people who are like that unnamed servant in the Church today. They will stay with you as long as the going is good but will disappear once you come under attack or stumble. Some of them will even stand with your enemies and slander you. Betrayal is real. Even the angels are surprised at how some people slander their men of God (Jude 1:8-10).

Many of Jesus' followers also left Him at one point (John 6). They remained with Him as long as they had plenty to eat and witness great miracles but fled at the first sign of attack. Few days ago, they wanted Him to be their king but today, they're shouting "Crucify Him". That's human being for you. White teeth don't indicate white heart. Someone can be kissing you and smiling while they're already negotiating with your enemies on how to sell you. Remember Judas? The heart of man is desperately wicked but God will reward everyone based on their heart and not their pretense; *"The heart is deceitful above all things, And desperately wicked; who can know it? I, the LORD, search the heart, I test the mind, Even to give every man according to his ways, According to the fruit of his doings"* (Jeremiah 17:9-10).

Elijah had no shoulder to lean upon in his trial period. Not one of those he has ministered to stood up for him. His armour bearer was nowhere close. Everyone he has labored upon abandoned him. He was depressed and wanted to die. How can anyone qualify for a double portion if they cannot endure the trials and trouble time with their Elijah?

Elijah felt so lonely in the wilderness while his supposed apprentice was comfortable in Beersheba.

You see, God had to replace such a disloyal servant with Elisha. It was in that wilderness experience that the Lord chose another armour bearer for Elijah (1Kings 19:16).

There is a spiritual law of replacement. God replaced Vashti with Esther (Esther 1-2), Saul with David (1Samuel 15:28) and Judas with Matthias (Acts 1:16-26). It is not always the one who gets there first that takes the mantle; it is the one whose heart is best.

There are times in ministry that the baton of leadership doesn't fall on the expected. Sometimes it is not by hierarchy but by favour. Honour is the seed you sow for favour. Passing the leadership baton or putting the wrong person in the position of authority can have a very devastating result. Many ministries have gone down because of politics and leadership appointments that are not God's will. We cannot side-track the Holy Spirit in His own business and expect no consequences.

Elisha understood honour and loyalty better than the unnamed servant. The Bible never even mentioned his name because it wasn't significant. The same Jezebel who threatened to kill Elijah eventually died a disgraceful death according to his prophecy (2Kings 9:30-37). God's prophets are not puppets to be toyed with, they're powerful! God is looking for loyal people to entrust His power into today.

ELISHA'S CALL

God has ordained from the ancient times that His grace be transferred and transmitted between and through human vessels. You see, it was the Lord who first called Elisha before he began pursuing Elijah and the double portion anointing.

You can only get the anointing that comes with the office that God has called you into. Elisha was a big time farmer and warrior before the Lord called him into ministry. The Lord told Elijah, *"Also you shall anoint Jehu the son of Nimshi as king over Israel. AND ELISHA THE SON OF SHAPHAT OF ABEL MEHOLAH YOU SHALL ANOINT AS PROPHET IN YOUR PLACE. It shall be that whoever escapes the sword of Hazael, Jehu will kill; and WHOEVER ESCAPES THE SWORD OF JEHU, ELISHA WILL KILL"* (1Kings 19:16-17).

Elijah did as the Lord instructed him and cast his mantle upon Elisha while he was ploughing. He wasn't an idle man. It is really difficult to find anyone in the Bible used by God who was idle; *"So he departed from there, and found Elisha the son of Shaphat, who was plowing with twelve yoke of oxen before him, and he was with the twelfth. Then Elijah passed by him and threw his mantle on him"* (1Kings 19:19).

An idle man cannot have the passion required for ministry. God is very passionate, He is always working and Jesus took after Him; *"But Jesus answered them, "My Father has been working until now, and I have been working""* (John 5:17).

Lazy people will not fulfill their ministry or complete their assignment. Paul had to send a message to a minister in that regard; *"Tell Archippus: "See to it that you complete the ministry you have received in the Lord""* (Colossians 4:17 NIV).

You see, the mantle that Elijah casted upon Elisha was a symbol of his call into ministry. It was the initial measure of the anointing but the bigger shot was still ahead of him. It was his responsibility to keep pressing and walking closely with his master and he did. It was up to him to complete his assignment and not fadeout on the way like the unnamed servant before him.

When God calls you, He gives you an initial anointing upon but that's not your destination. You're supposed to keep pressing deeper and walking faithfully so that a greater one can be entrusted to you.

Many do not really go beyond that initial anointing. They get complacent once ministry begins to yield little financial profit. They're lost in the comfort zone and distracted by material things and the praise of men. The double portion anointing doesn't come cheaply.

Elijah didn't want Elisha to go back and kiss his dad; *"And he left the oxen and ran after Elijah, and said, "Please let me kiss my father and my mother, and then I will follow you." And he said to him, "Go back again, for what have I done to you?"* (1Kings 19:20). Jesus says that no one can follow Him if they do not love Him more than their family (Luke 14:26).

The anointing is not for those who are not willing to leave everything behind. It is a huge responsibility.

THE TRANSFERENCE OF SPIRITS

In fact, Elisha got the double portion because he was very determined. When he received the call into the ministry, he destroyed everything he was ploughing with. He renounced his former life and was fully ready to follow God. God will not take a second place in your life; *"So Elisha turned back from him, and took a yoke of oxen and slaughtered them and boiled their flesh, using the oxen's equipment, and gave it to the people, and they ate. Then he arose and followed Elijah, and became his servant"* (1Kings 19:21).

Elisha destroyed everything that could have tempted him to go back. He accepted the call with great joy and even celebrated it with a feast. The call of God brings joy. How much are you willing to sacrifice for the anointing?

Watch closely how that Elisha was so much spiritually and physically in tune with his master Elijah as we examine some Bible passages;

2KINGS 2:1-8
1 ¶ And it came to pass, when the LORD was about to take up Elijah into heaven by a whirlwind, that Elijah went with Elisha from Gilgal.

2 Then Elijah said to Elisha, "Stay here, please, for the LORD has sent me on to Bethel." But Elisha said, "AS THE LORD LIVES, AND AS YOUR SOUL LIVES, I WILL NOT LEAVE YOU!" SO THEY WENT DOWN TO BETHEL.

3 Now the sons of the prophets who were at Bethel came out to Elisha, and said to him, "Do you know that the LORD will take away your master from over you today?" And he said, "Yes, I know; keep silent!"

4 Then Elijah said to him, "Elisha, stay here, please, for the LORD has sent me on to Jericho." But he said, "AS THE LORD LIVES, AND AS YOUR SOUL LIVES, I WILL NOT LEAVE YOU!" SO THEY CAME TO JERICHO.

5 Now the sons of the prophets who were at Jericho came to Elisha and said to him, "Do you know that the LORD will take away your master from over you today?" So he answered, "Yes, I know; keep silent!"

6 Then Elijah said to him, "Stay here, please, for the LORD has sent me on to the Jordan." But he said, "AS THE LORD LIVES, AND AS YOUR SOUL LIVES, I WILL NOT LEAVE YOU!" SO THE TWO OF THEM WENT ON.

7 And fifty men of the sons of the prophets went and stood facing them at a distance, while the two of them stood by the Jordan.

8 Now Elijah took his mantle, rolled it up, and struck the water; and it was divided this way and that, so that the two of them crossed over on dry ground.

SPIRITUALLY IN TUNE

Notice two very important things in the previous passage. The first is that Elisha walked closely with his master and will not leave him for any cause. And secondly, it wasn't the other sons of the prophets that had to tell him of his master's departure. It did not come to him as a shock but rather, he had also gotten it in the spirit realm already because he was spiritually in tune with God and also with his master.

Many today are so disloyal to their spiritual parents. I've seen a lot who are like Absalom. They want the anointing so they can divide their father's "kingdom". They want to pull half of the congregation away. They're not willing to serve or wait upon the Lord. They want everything very fast. Their eyes is on their father's "throne", they're envious of his position and will gladly overthrow him.

The reason many submit to a ministry is not to serve but to takeover. Their passion is not for the Lord but for the profit of ministry. Their heart is full of greed and obsession with power, fame and popularity.

Just because you have a little taste of the anointing doesn't mean you should pull out half-baked to float your own ministry without your father's blessing or God's approval. Those who skip the making process because they cannot endure do not last in ministry. Only those who can endure training will enjoy reigning and last.

Elisha touched Elijah's heart with his loyalty before he could access his anointing.

If you can't touch your father's heart, you cannot access his gift or anointing.

Elisha didn't follow Elijah for a day and received the double portion the following morning. His heart was proven over the years. He was a hard follower.

He didn't see himself as a colleague prophet. The anointing doesn't really flow upward or sideways but downwards.

The anointing on Aaron flowed from his head down to his beards and garment, not the other way round; *"For harmony is as precious as the anointing oil that was poured over Aaron's head, that ran down his beard and onto the border of his robe"* (Psalm 133:2 NLT).

If you put yourself on the same level with your Elijah, his anointing will not flow sideways to you. If you exalt yourself above him, it will not flow upwards to you. Only those who humble themselves under will receive the unction because it only flows downwards.

Elisha served as a faithful armour bearer. In fact he was first popular for pouring water on Elijah's hands before becoming famous for being a prophet; *"But Jehoshaphat asked, "Is there no prophet of the LORD here, through whom we may inquire of the LORD?" An officer of the king of Israel answered, "ELISHA SON OF SHAPHAT IS HERE. HE USED TO POUR WATER ON THE HANDS OF ELIJAH""* (2Kings 3:11 NIV).

If you cannot humble yourself to pour water on the prophet's hands, you will not get the double portion anointing.

OFFENDED OR ANOINTED?

Elijah seemed to be pushing Elisha away but that young man was too smart to go away. He kept telling him to wait behind but the young man wouldn't let him out of sight for a second.

Have you ever drawn close to a man of God who has something that you need but also with an attitude that pushes away? Don't let offences cheat you out of God's best for your life.

There's something you need in someone you don't find flawless.

God anoints imperfect people. Learn from Elisha's wisdom and refuse to be turned off. The double portion is not going to come from a prophet you're offended at. Are you offended or anointed?

Elisha was a faithful son and servant of his spiritual father. He loved him and would not leave him no matter what. Even when Elijah asked him to wait, he told him plainly that he would go on with him no matter what. He was ready to continue with his

THE TRANSFERENCE OF SPIRITS

master until the very end and he did. He followed him in all conditions.

Elisha's undying persistency and undeniable loyalty caused Elijah to ask of Elisha what should be done for him.

The master was so impressed by this addicted follower. He has tested his faithfulness and has found him worthy of an honour. Consequently, he perceived that he must have a desire, and asked him for what he desired. His reply was a double portion of his father's spirit.

Elisha could have asked for the properties that Elijah left behind but he was mindful of spiritual things. His heart was not in gold like Gehazi. He knew that what he would eat was not as important as what he would be.

It is not easy serving a master who is capable of roasting battalions with his anointing (2Kings 1:9-12) but Elisha was a wise and patient apprentice. Is your heart qualified for a double portion?

A DOUBLE PORTION WILL NOT COME CHEAPLY

2KINGS 2:9-10

9 ¶ And so it was, when they had crossed over, that Elijah said to Elisha, "Ask! What may I do for you, before I am taken away from you?" Elisha said, "PLEASE LET A DOUBLE PORTION OF YOUR SPIRIT BE UPON ME."

10 So he said, "You have asked a hard thing. Nevertheless, if you see me when I am taken from you, it shall be so for you; but if not, it shall not be so.

Elisha would get his desired request, yet, there was still a final test, the one that this son must not fail in order to earn his earnest desire. He must be spiritually alert enough. He must be closely connected enough and he must be spiritually sensitive enough to see his father when he is being received up. Spiritual vision requires intimacy. Jesus was not transfigured before the whole world. Only Peter, James and John witnessed it (Mathew 17).

Elisha made it because his heart was with his master. They were so intimate in a spiritual sense. He honoured him and called him father. This young man understood intimacy without disrespect.

THE TRANSFERENCE OF SPIRITS

You see, it is not everyone that can handle intimacy. Some folks will stop honouring you the day they're allowed into your house. Elisha saw the humanity and weaknesses of the man who could call fire down. Yet, he honoured him;

2KINGS 2:11-15
11 Then it happened, as they continued on and talked, that suddenly a chariot of fire appeared with horses of fire, and separated the two of them; and Elijah went up by a whirlwind into heaven.
12 And Elisha saw it, and he cried out, "MY FATHER, MY FATHER, THE CHARIOT OF ISRAEL AND ITS HORSEMEN!" So he saw him no more. And he took hold of his own clothes and tore them into two pieces.
13 ¶ He also took up the mantle of Elijah that had fallen from him, and went back and stood by the bank of the Jordan.
14 Then he took the mantle of Elijah that had fallen from him, and struck the water, and said, "Where is the LORD God of Elijah?" And when he also had struck the water, it was divided this way and that; and Elisha crossed over.
15 Now when the sons of the prophets who were from Jericho saw him, they said, "THE SPIRIT OF ELIJAH RESTS ON ELISHA." AND THEY CAME TO MEET HIM, AND BOWED TO THE GROUND BEFORE HIM.

THE ANOINTING IS NOT FOR MOCKERS

The sons of the prophets who mocked Elisha got nothing. However, they bowed when the man who would not criticize or dishonour his father but celebrate the unction upon him came back with the mantle of his twain spirit.

Elijah's last miracle became Elisha's first when he parted the sea with the mantle of his father, who had divided it earlier; *"He also took up the mantle of Elijah that had fallen from him, and went back and stood by the bank of the Jordan. Then he took the mantle of Elijah that had fallen from him, and struck the water, and said, "Where is the LORD God of Elijah?" And when he also had struck the water, it was divided this way and that; and Elisha crossed over"* (2Kings 2:13-14).

His father's mantle worked in his hand because his heart was genuinely connected.

You see, if it were one of those jester sons of the prophets that took the mantle, struck the water and shouted "Where is the LORD God of Elijah?", nothing would have happened. The prophet's mantle only answers to genuine faith heart connection.

I remember the testimony of one of my loyal spiritual daughters who is now a Barrister. While she was in the University, a certain lecturer vowed that she would not graduate unless she let him sleep with her. She refused and the man started failing her in his courses.

Eventually, when the man wouldn't let her graduate, she said she went on her knees and cried out to God saying; "God of my father Samson Ajilore, arise for my defence." That was all!

The next thing that followed was an apology from the lecturer. She even showed me one of the text messages the man had sent to her.

It was that same man who later went round and rectified her papers.

The God of the prophet that you mock in the secret will not defend you in the open and the God of the prophet you honour will not ignore you in trouble.

Notice that Elijah followed Elisha so closely and learn the ways of a prophet with a sincere heart. You must be willing to follow the ministry that carries what you desire.

Some can just stay around the anointed and get imparted but the real transference of spirit requires a strong heart connection and loyalty.

The anointing is not for the arrogant or wonderers. It is for those who are willing to stay with the anointed and serve with a pure heart.

Several sit back in the Church today, criticizing every move of God and causing damage and wounds in the body.

The enemy is using them without them even knowing it, and he is using them against the body they are supposed to build.

The anointing we attack, we cannot attract. Only what we appreciate can be apprehended. The reason some folks cannot receive the anointing is an attitude of dishonor.

ELISHA AND GEHAZI

Elisha got a double portion because his heart was with his father and master. The mantle of his master parted the waters in his hands the same way it did in his master's hand.

On the other hand, the same staff or rod that worked for the prophet Elisha did not work in the hand of Gehazi his greedy apprentice, when he was to use it to raise a child back to life from the dead. I believe that the reason was because his heart was not with his master;

2 KINGS 4:29-31
29 Then he said to Gehazi, "Get yourself ready, and take my staff in your hand, and be on your way. If you meet anyone, do not greet him; and if anyone greets you, do not answer him; but lay my staff on the face of the child."
30 And the mother of the child said, "As the LORD lives, and as your soul lives, I will not leave you." So he arose and followed her.
31 Now Gehazi went on ahead of them, and laid the staff on the face of the child; but there was neither voice nor hearing. Therefore he went back to meet

him, and told him, saying, "The child has not awakened."

What is working for your prophet will not work for you if your heart is not with him. Disloyal servants make their master's anointing appear irrelevant. The Yoruba people use to say that, "Abiku so oloogun di eke". That means a demonic child that is bond to death puts the physician to shame by defying all medications.

Sometimes, you wonder why the same spiritual approach that worked for one person will prove abortive with another. Most times, the difference is in the heart of the people that you're ministering to.

The anointing sometimes refuses to work for rebellious people because their heart is not right. It is a dangerous thing to walk in rebellion against God or His servants.

If you cannot touch a prophet's heart, you may not be able to access his anointing. The heart is everything with God; *"My son, give me your heart, And let your eyes observe my ways"* (Proverbs 23:26). God wants your heart!

Spiritual intimacy is so visible between Elijah and Elisha and it is necessary for such transference. However, intimacy with humans without intimacy with God will end up in idolatry and corruption.

If a spiritual connection is genuine, the mark of its genuineness will be the evidence that follows the incident, the demonstration of power and the progressive fruits that follow the impartation of grace. All must however be to the glory of Christ.

If we are the body of Christ, how else will He shine if not through us?

It is time to let Him shine through us to the glory and praise of God the Father! *"Let your light so shine before men, that they may see your good works and glorify your Father in heaven"* (Mathew 5:16). We have the responsibility of shining God's light into the darkness that's in this world. God cannot reveal His glory to the world without going through the Church. Our lack of cooperation is slowing down His work.

GENERATIONAL MANTLES

In this Kingdom, there are generational mantles lying down for us to enter. Joshua entered that of Moses. Elisha entered that of Elijah. John the Baptist came in the spirit and power of Elijah. I believe that a person do not have to join the cloud of witnesses before the grace of God upon him can be reproduced upon others. In addition, more than one person can also partake of the anointing of God upon a person. Seventy elders partook of the spirit of the man Moses and it was in his life time;

NUMBERS 11:16-30 (KJV)
16 ¶ And the LORD said unto Moses, Gather unto me seventy men of the elders of Israel, whom thou knowest to be the elders of the people, and officers over them; and bring them unto the tabernacle of the congregation, that they may stand there with thee.
17 AND I WILL COME DOWN AND TALK WITH THEE THERE: AND I WILL TAKE OF THE SPIRIT WHICH IS UPON THEE, AND WILL PUT IT UPON THEM; AND THEY SHALL BEAR THE BURDEN OF THE PEOPLE WITH THEE, THAT THOU BEAR IT NOT THYSELF ALONE.
18 And say thou unto the people, Sanctify yourselves against to morrow, and ye shall eat flesh: for ye have

THE TRANSFERENCE OF SPIRITS

wept in the ears of the LORD, saying, Who shall give us flesh to eat? for it was well with us in Egypt: therefore the LORD will give you flesh, and ye shall eat.

19 Ye shall not eat one day, nor two days, nor five days, neither ten days, nor twenty days;

20 But even a whole month, until it come out at your nostrils, and it be loathsome unto you: because that ye have despised the LORD which is among you, and have wept before him, saying, Why came we forth out of Egypt? {whole...: Heb. month of days}

21 And Moses said, The people, among whom I am, are six hundred thousand footmen; and thou hast said, I will give them flesh, that they may eat a whole month.

22 Shall the flocks and the herds be slain for them, to suffice them? or shall all the fish of the sea be gathered together for them, to suffice them?

23 And the LORD said unto Moses, Is the LORD'S hand waxed short? thou shalt see now whether my word shall come to pass unto thee or not.

24 ¶ And Moses went out, and told the people the words of the LORD, and gathered the seventy men of the elders of the people, and set them round about the tabernacle.

25 AND THE LORD CAME DOWN IN A CLOUD, AND SPAKE UNTO HIM, AND TOOK OF THE SPIRIT THAT WAS UPON HIM, AND GAVE IT UNTO THE SEVENTY ELDERS: AND IT CAME TO PASS, THAT, WHEN THE

SPIRIT RESTED UPON THEM, THEY PROPHESIED, AND DID NOT CEASE.

26 BUT THERE REMAINED TWO OF THE MEN IN THE CAMP, THE NAME OF THE ONE WAS ELDAD, AND THE NAME OF THE OTHER MEDAD: AND THE SPIRIT RESTED UPON THEM; AND THEY WERE OF THEM THAT WERE WRITTEN, BUT WENT NOT OUT UNTO THE TABERNACLE: AND THEY PROPHESIED IN THE CAMP.

27 And there ran a young man, and told Moses, and said, Eldad and Medad do prophesy in the camp.

28 And Joshua the son of Nun, the servant of Moses, one of his young men, answered and said, My lord Moses, forbid them.

29 And Moses said unto him, Enviest thou for my sake? WOULD GOD THAT ALL THE LORD'S PEOPLE WERE PROPHETS, AND THAT THE LORD WOULD PUT HIS SPIRIT UPON THEM!

30 And Moses gat him into the camp, he and the elders of Israel.

It is clear throughout the Scripture and Church history that God is the originator of the transference of spirits. He wants many in this generation to enter those mantles and advance His Kingdom on earth. I got to my mail box one morning and saw the news from Charisma Magazine that Oral Roberts graduated to be with the Lord four days earlier, at the age of ninety one. He was a man whose ministry has blessed the body of Christ tremendously for several decades. There must be someone or certain people, who will enter into the mantle of such a man, yet it would not randomly fall on anyone. It takes faith and true spiritual connection to get it. Oral was a great healing evangelist and also a great man of prayer, who showed millions the way of Christ. I remember how blessed I was after reading his autobiography, "My life and ministry." He was so anointed that his hand will vibrate with the healing anointing uncontrollably.

Mantles are lying down throughout the centuries for kingdom advancement. The mantles that centuries have dropped are crowding the hours of the setting sun, for men and women must enter them and advance the kingdom, as we approach the consummation of this present age. God taught me that He often let the teachings of these great men and women in the kingdom circulate exceedingly, the moment they join the cloud of witness, so that their mantles will be taken hold by those that will soak in those teachings.

ENTERING INTO THE MANTLES

NUMBERS 11:16-17

16 ¶ So the LORD said to Moses: "Gather to Me seventy men of the elders of Israel, whom you know to be the elders of the people and officers over them; bring them to the tabernacle of meeting, that they may stand there with you.

17 "Then I will come down and talk with you there. I will take of the Spirit that is upon you and will put the same upon them; and they shall bear the burden of the people with you, that you may not bear it yourself alone.

ACTS 3:25

25 "You are sons of the prophets, and of the covenant which God made with our fathers, saying to Abraham, 'And in your seed all the families of the earth shall be blessed.

We can enter into the mantles of men and women who are ahead of us in the ministry of the Word and prayers and thus, advance even better than them.

However, it is not filling the shoes of others but fully filling our own individual unique destinies in our generations. We can start from where they stop.

The transference of spirits is real. True servants receive the double portion anointing and true sons and daughters in the Kingdom take after their parents.

I minister today from a measure of the anointing of God upon several generals of faith, both home and abroad, most of whom have since joined the cloud of witnesses.

These people are not dead; they are alive. Zoë, the life that God gives to us in Christ is immortal. Since God our Father is immortal, we, His children are also immortal spirits (Hebrews 12:9).

I have desired greatly the grace upon certain men and women of God and as a matter of fact, a lot of people have named me after some of them.

I have read their books day and night, over and again, listened to their messages times without number and watched their videos times and again. I soaked in them, fastened my spirit tenaciously to them, poured over them and prayed in the Holy Spirit for transference of grace until something from them rubbed off on me.

I found out that I have become more enriched and could minister from a measure of their spirits (the anointing is a spirit: by this, I imply the power of God).

I am a combination of varieties of God's grace and I am bold to declare this because the Word says that we are members of one another and so, we all are joined to the Lord and we are one Spirit with Him (Ephesians 4:25; 1 Corinthians 6:17).

We can connect with the same grace that is upon a minister or their ministry, God is not bound to one person or denomination.

God doesn't want us to be rigid or dogmatic. We must be open to the leading of the Spirit in whatever way He would direct us, even though unorthodox to us. As long as it is biblical! We're not supposed to fight or reject everything that we do not understand. Deception is whatever the Bible is opposed to, not what our personal believe is against.

THE SPIRITS OF JUST MEN MADE PERFECT
HEBREWS 12:22-24
**22 But you have come to Mount Zion and to the city of the living God, the heavenly Jerusalem, to an innumerable company of angels,
23 to the general assembly and Church of the firstborn who are registered in heaven, to God the Judge of all, TO THE SPIRITS OF JUST MEN MADE PERFECT,
24 to Jesus the Mediator of the new covenant, and to the blood of sprinkling that speaks better things than that of Abel.**

The previous passage says that we have come unto the spirits of just men made perfect and unto Jesus the Mediator of the New Covenant among other things.

The spirit of just men made perfect surrounds us today; they are around us in the spirit realm. There is no distance over there and they see us as we run our race.

They are the great cloud of witnesses that encircles us round about. I believe that they were the cloud that received Jesus up to heaven; *"Now when He had spoken these things, while they watched, He was* taken up, and *A CLOUD RECEIVED HIM OUT OF THEIR SIGHT"* (Acts 1:9).

Hebrews 12:1 calls them the great cloud of witnesses; *"Therefore we also, since WE ARE SURROUNDED BY SO GREAT A CLOUD OF WITNESSES, let us lay aside every weight, and the sin which so easily ensnares us, and let us run with endurance the race that is set before us."*

These saints surround us in the spirit realm, watching as we run our own individual races. They're like spectators in our life's game. They've concluded their own journey, now, they behold as we take ours.

Moses and Elijah appeared and were talking with the Lord Jesus on the mountain of transfiguration. He came to fulfil the law and the prophets. Moses signifies the law and Elijah signifies the prophets (Mark 9:4).

Two men also stood before the disciples when Jesus was received up to heaven, the spirits of the just men made perfect are still very active today (Acts 1:10).

THE TRANSFERENCE OF SPIRITS

The anointing is a spirit and it is contagious, communicable and transferable (Numbers 11:17; 25; 2 Kings 2:9, 15).

God still uses certain personalities, most especially those with our kinds of ministry to equip and empower us.

We are all spirit beings and He is the Father of spirits; the holy living spirits, known and unknown, seen and unseen. All the ones on earth and those in heaven. He determines how spirits operates (Hebrews 12:9, Numbers 16:22).

Our life is by God's design and purpose, and He keeps reproducing those anointing and multiplying them upon the Church folds. Since, they are only necessary for the saints upon the earth to advance the Kingdom. The anointing is not needed in heaven. No sickness to heal or demons to cast out over there. Mantles must go from one generation to another in the Church.

CHAPTER 4

CAUTIONS!

"Imitate me, just as I also imitate Christ"
-1 Corinthians 11:1.

We know from the Scriptures that, following close after someone is the way to get the anointing upon their life and also that the anointing increases through association (2 Kings 2; 1 Samuel 10:5-6). Nevertheless, we should also know that the anointing obtainable for us is the one for the office into which we have already obtained a divine calling of God.

For example, an evangelist cannot obtain a prophets' mantle, neither can a teacher obtain the mantle of an apostle if God has not divinely called him into that office. The anointing we pursue should be that on the head of someone who has the same calling with us.

LESSONS FROM SAUL AND MIRIAM

Notice that you won't have to strain yourself to do your calling because it is within your ability.

When you step into another person's calling, you will struggle fruitlessly.

A good example of this is the King Saul. He was only a king, not a prophet or priest. Saul's downfall came when he FORCED himself out of fear to perform a sacrifice which was only within the power and office of Samuel who was both a prophet and priest to do;

1SAMUEL 13:7-14 (KJV)
7 And [some of] the Hebrews went over Jordan to the land of Gad and Gilead. As for Saul, he [was] yet in Gilgal, and all the people followed him trembling.

THE TRANSFERENCE OF SPIRITS

8 And he tarried seven days, according to the set time that Samuel [had appointed]: but Samuel came not to Gilgal; and the people were scattered from him.

9 And Saul said, Bring hither a burnt offering to me, and peace offerings. And he offered the burnt offering.

10 And it came to pass, that as soon as he had made an end of offering the burnt offering, behold, Samuel came; and Saul went out to meet him, that he might salute him.

11 And Samuel said, What hast thou done? And Saul said, Because I saw that the people were scattered from me, and [that] thou camest not within the days appointed, and [that] the Philistines gathered themselves together at Michmash;

12 THEREFORE SAID I, THE PHILISTINES WILL COME DOWN NOW UPON ME TO GILGAL, AND I HAVE NOT MADE SUPPLICATION UNTO THE LORD: I FORCED MYSELF THEREFORE, AND OFFERED A BURNT OFFERING.

13 And Samuel said to Saul, Thou hast done foolishly: thou hast not kept the commandment of the LORD thy God, which he commanded thee: for now would the LORD have established thy kingdom upon Israel for ever.

14 But now thy kingdom shall not continue: the LORD hath sought him a man after his own heart, and the LORD hath commanded him [to be] captain over his

people, because thou hast not kept [that] which the LORD commanded thee.

Never let fear, greed or pressure force you into another person's office. Stay within your calling and be faithful to it. Your anointing, ability and productivity only lies within the sphere of your calling.

Miriam also met leprosy when she stepped outside of her calling and began to scold Moses, a spiritual superior (Numbers 12). Her ministry started going down from that day until nothing was practically heard of her again. So many people and ministries have gone down because of careless words. If you want to be a lasting voice and enjoy longevity in ministry, stay in your own calling.

You see, that popular expression, mind your own business is originally a Bible commandment. *"...ALSO ASPIRE TO LEAD A QUIET LIFE, TO MIND YOUR OWN BUSINESS, AND TO WORK WITH YOUR OWN HANDS, as we commanded you"* (1 Thessalonians 4:11).

Don't poke your nose into the affairs of other ministers and their ministries. Stay where the Lord has placed you. Nothing good awaits you outside your anointing except spiritual leprosy. And, that will make those who used to love you to start resenting you. We really have to be careful of how we speak of the Lord's anointed and what we get involved in. Even the angels are careful with their words (Jude 1:8-10).

DON'T DUPLICATE AN ERROR
JUDE 1:11
11 Woe to them! For they have gone in the way of Cain, have run greedily in the error of Balaam for profit, and perished in the rebellion of Korah.

You see, we must be careful that those people whose faith we imitate do not replace God in our hearts. And also, that we do not reproduce their weaknesses or mistakes. One of the challenges of discipleship relationship is that, a disciple can become blind to the blind spots of his master and begin to reproduce his mistakes. Another caution is that we must not follow people beyond the extent to which they follow God. As Kenneth E Hagin would say, "If he (the fellow you are following) misses it a little, do not follow that little."

We should only be imitators of people as they imitate Christ. Then we should also be watchful for some dangers like dying at the same age that the person we follow dies.

Kenneth E. Hagin followed Smith Wigglesworth so closely, (although it was only through studying his writings) and he did that so much, literally wearing his books out, until something of Smith robbed off on him. We know that Hagin graduated to be with the Lord at the age of 86; one year behind Wigglesworth. That was pretty close!

Now, someone could follow a leader who died at a very young age and also die at that age too. He could even have the same sickness that the leader had and duplicate several other negative things.

I remember some years back, when the Lord asked me to travel to a particular town in another state and correct a very great prophetic friend. This man of God had told his wife that he would go to be with the Lord at age fifty. He had received abundant revelations of heaven and had followed so closely after a certain man who taught that there is nothing to live for on the earth.

You see, people can become so heavenly conscious that they will become so "earthly useless". I mean in the negative side, because there is also a positive side to this. If God doesn't want us on earth, why didn't He transport us to heaven the day we got saved? The truth is that even the millennium reign will be on earth because God has given the earth to the sons of men and the righteous will inherit it (Psalm 37:9).

When I got through taking that dear brother through the Word, he called his wife and made a declaration that she should no longer prepare to be a widow on his 50th birthday, but that they will both live to a full old age. The Word of God must not be replaced by the doctrines of our fathers or mentors.

Often, when leaders get off the Word and end up in certain difficulties, their followers are blind to it because they are caught up in the anointing upon their lives and ministry. Yet, the anointing is not the stamp that makes whatever a person does or says right. In fact, one could propound errors while the anointing is still upon one's head. And, such errors will go far to cause great damage because people will consume them for the sake of one's anointing. Some of the greatest errors in the history of the Church have been introduced by some of the most anointed men and women.

THE FAST FOOD SYNDROME!

God doesn't want us to remain spiritual babes who cannot comprehend spiritual things or even discern what He is doing among us;

HEBREWS 5:11-14
11 of whom we have much to say, and hard to explain, since you have become dull of hearing.
12 For though by this time you ought to be teachers, you need someone to teach you again the first principles of the oracles of God; and you have come to need milk and not solid food.
13 For everyone who partakes only of milk is unskilled in the word of righteousness, for he is a babe.

14 But solid food belongs to those who are of full age, that is, those who by reason of use have their senses exercised to discern both good and evil.

There must be a perfect blend of the Spirit and the Word in these last days.

The Church must go back to Berea.

The Berean believers sat under one of the most anointed men in their time. They were under Paul, a man whom many have ranked only next to Christ in works and revelations. Yet, unlike many Christians today, they did not just consume all that he said and were not caught up in the miracles that he performed. But, they searched the Scriptures which they had then, to ensure that everything that this Apostle taught them was correct. It was for that singular act that God said they were noble;

ACTS 17:10-12 (KJV)
10 ¶ And the brethren immediately sent away Paul and Silas by night unto Berea: who coming thither went into the synagogue of the Jews.
11 These were more noble than those in Thessalonica, in that they received the word with all readiness of

mind, and searched the scriptures daily, whether those things were so.
12 Therefore many of them believed; also of honourable women which were Greeks, and of men, not a few.

Isn't it amazing that God's choice of nobility is quite different from ours?

I wonder how many noble Christians we have today in such a time as this, when the fast food syndrome has eaten deep into the Church like a cankerworm, and many do not hold sound doctrines any more.

We now have several goose bump Christians, who are not rooted and grounded in the Word, but want everything fast, including a fifteen minutes sermon on a Sunday service.

No wonder many of us are so shallow, including the ministers. That's why our results are also shallow.

God wants us to be far deeper than we can ever imagine!

MERE DESIRE IS NOT ENOUGH

We desire greater results than the days of men like Charles G. Finney, but several of those old saints would often preach a sermon of about three hours before embarking on other ministrations. Contrary to some of our prophets today, who would just get into the pulpit and start calling out people and giving them words from the Lord, without any sermon! Thus, we build babes and think that such a Church would stand. A pastor might have to preach to the chairs if his sermon goes beyond thirty minutes in some of our Churches today.

The Lord has shown me by revelations that He is bringing up more prophet teachers in the body of Christ who will bring a balance between sound doctrines and visions, to advance the Church to maturity. God usually moves in His Word and when people hear it, the Spirit follows it; *"While Peter was still speaking these words, the Holy Spirit fell upon all those who heard the word"* (Acts 10:44). That sounds like the Spirit interrupted Peter's sermon. How much we need that today! The same Holy Spirit is in us and He must be allowed to produce the proof of what we preach.

TARRYING FOR THE GLORY

People no longer want to tarry in God's presence, yet, they want the glory to come down. Majority of us are too caught up in Church and business things, but are far removed from the presence; the secret place.

Many of us never even press beyond the first veil because we never do anything beyond the soul realm. We are so concerned about our intellectual abilities with words well chosen to appeal to human minds so as to attract clapping ovation and we are satisfied.

You see, there is a greater glory behind the veil and it is open to us by the blood of Christ (Hebrews 10:19-20), but it is our duty to come in. We sometimes need God to interrupt our schedules and establish His own pattern in our worship lives so that we will stop having "our" service and doing "our" Church, but start having His service and doing His Church.

Smith Wigglesworth used to consider his dressing incomplete without a Bible during his earthly days. He would never go out without his pocket size Bible. Each time he eats, whether in the public restaurant or in any other place at all, he would reach forth his hand and pull out his small Bible and say, the meal is not complete without feeding the spirit, for man shall not live by bread alone but by every Word of God.

No wonder he was such a radical man of great faith.

Several believers today will feed their belly full with so much natural food and leave their spirit starving, only to feed it in some shallow Sunday morning snack, once in a week.

That is why many live a life of defeat and mediocrity, appearing great in the natural but being so weakly in the spirit.

Just the way the natural body will not function well without natural food, the human spirit will malfunction without good spiritual nourishment.

WAR AGAINST RELIGIOUS SPIRITS

"And no wonder! For Satan himself transforms himself into an angel of light. Therefore it is no great thing if his ministers also transform themselves into ministers of righteousness, whose end will be according to their works"
-2Corinthians 11:14-15.

Christianity is not another religion, it is a relationship. Religion is fallen human's attempt to reach God but Christianity is God's resolution to reach humanity. Religion will fail but Christianity will not!

MATHEW 23:29
29 "Woe to you, scribes and Pharisees, hypocrites! Because you build the tombs of the prophets and adorn the monuments of the righteous.

LUKE 12:56
56 Hypocrites! You can discern the face of the sky and of the earth, but how is it you do not discern this time?

2TIMOTHY 3:5
5 having a form of godliness but denying its power. And from such people turn away!

THE TRANSFERENCE OF SPIRITS

A religious spirit is a spirit that appreciates, celebrates and publicizes where God has been. It embraces the past moves of God, the great saints that have joined the cloud of witnesses but will not recognize, welcome, accept and appreciate where God is. It frowns at the present move of God and His current works in our midst.

This spirit rejects the present saints of God that are being used today, including those in the fivefold ministry and the others.

This spirit has been sent from the pit of hell so as to keep us living in history and be kept back from prophecy. And, so that we may fail to recognize those that the Lord is raising in our midst today.

This is the spirit of the old guards; old members of the Church fold that are often opposed to a change.

The God of the Bible is not bound to the ancient past or the distant future; He is operating in the now. The move of God is for today and everything that we have read and heard of can still be experienced today.

JESUS IS STILL THE SAME TODAY

God has not changed. Jesus Christ is the same yesterday, today and forever. What God wants to do today and tomorrow is greater than what He did yesterday and in the past. We must stand against religious spirits and yield to the Spirit of truth for only the truth can set us free. True freedom comes from the knowledge of the truth. The degree of the truth that we know will be in the right proportion to the freedom we enjoy. God's Word is the truth (John 17:17).

There are folks in the Church today who have been saved for long but are very difficult for the Holy Spirit to work through. I've noticed that it is much easier to minister the baptism with the Holy Spirit to young folks than to many of those old Church people. The children are quick to believe but many adults often reason away the Spirit, they let their brain get in the way of their heart. No wonder Jesus thanked the Father for keeping the things of the Kingdom away from those who are wise in their own eyes and revealing them to kids; "In that hour Jesus rejoiced in the Spirit and said, *"I thank You, Father, Lord of heaven and earth, that You have hidden these things from the wise and prudent and revealed them to babes. Even so, Father, for so it seemed good in your sight"* (Luke 10:21). You can't use your brain to analyze everything; the Holy Spirit is not a biology class. Spiritual things are not like physical ones. Faith will connect you to the supernatural!

That reminds me of a story I heard from a taped message by Corrie Ten Boom. She spoke about a time when someone asked her if she believed that Jonah was truly in the stomach of the whale as the Bible testified. She answered that she did not only believe it to be the truth but she would have believed also should the Bible had said that the whale was in the belly of Jonah because it is the Bible. No wonder she did so much exploits of faith for God. Jesus thanked the Father for keeping the mysteries of the Kingdom hidden from intellectual folks and revealing it to babes-simple minded people, because it pleased Him to do so (Mathew 11:25; Luke 10:21).

Childlike faith is a necessity for accessing the revelatory and transforming realms of the Word of God to provoke the supernatural in our day to day Christian life. It is the way to be naturally supernatural!

Chapter 5

THE LORD TAUGHT ME

"Whom will he teach knowledge? And whom will he make to understand the message? Those just weaned from milk? Those just drawn from the breasts? For precept must be upon precept, precept upon precept, Line upon line, line upon line, Here a little, there a little"
-Isaiah 28:9-10.

My maternal grandparents taught me against religious spirits from the Word of God and their experience in more than fifty-three years of ministry. I can say so much concerning their lives and ministries. Nevertheless, the summary is: they gave themselves fully to the ministry of the Word and prayer and they manifested the power and character of Christ. They were lovers.

The Lord later began teaching me even more about discernment and spiritual authority. Especially, on casting out devils and healing the sick. This started in prolonged visions beginning from the age of eight, when I got filled with the Holy Spirit in a Church where my grandfather was a pastor at the time.

My earliest days of passion for the Lord were characterized with a strong burden for souls. That drove me to the place of intercessory prayers and beyond the four corners of my streets. I would intercede and go out and tell people about the Lord. My cousin Isaac and I sometimes go together to preach the gospel to the people. I remember how he would interpret for me. I can't forget how I used to go even into classrooms and preach in the High School that I attended.

Those days, when Grandpa would take me to the farm on holidays, I would preach to the farmers, the birds of the air, the land animals, and to the wild forest. I can remember singing and making melody to God in my spirit and even singing my prayers with tears to the Father in worship, making my request known through thanksgiving. I just love Him. Every demon in hell knows that I love the Lord!

SNEAKING OUT OF SCHOOL TO PREACH

I like sharing my personal testimonies to the glory of God and to the edification of the saints. I used to leave school to preach in a university campus that was not too far from the High School that I attended.

I was writing tracts manually initially. Nevertheless, during my third year in the school, I had learned to trek a few kilometers home from school and also to go on fasting. This was so that I could save the money that was meant for my feeding and transportation, for printing my evangelistic tracts. My first title was, "You must be born again," and the second was, "Love not the world."

God began crowning my efforts when certain Muslims who had computer business centers would design and print my tracts free of charge. Then I would add up the money which I should have paid them to the photocopy bill.

During school hours, I would preach in the library and the students will gather in their numbers to listen. Many of them would even sit on the bare floor to hear God's Word, as I always taught from the gospels. Sometimes, the school Principal would come and dismiss us, he was a fine Muslim man.

On a regular basis, I was driven by my burden for souls so much that I would go and preach in the University campus during break times. And, even overspend the time in preaching. It was a great struggle for me to balance my passion for the gospel with my desire to learn in school, since I was almost always reading the Scriptures in the classroom. Sometimes, I used to hide my Bible under my locker and read from there when a teacher was in the class. I would even pray that the teacher would not catch me, so that I don't get punished or driven out of class.

Those were some of my extremes in those days, but I really loved the Lord. Like the young prophet Jeremiah, the Word of God was burning like fire in my heart and bones (Jeremiah 20:9).

It has always been my serious passion to keep my first love for Lord. This often takes me on personal spiritual retreats.

THE HOLY SPIRIT MY BEST FRIEND
"If you love Me, keep My commandments. And I will pray the Father, and He will give you another Helper, that He may abide with you forever--the Spirit of truth, whom the world cannot receive, because it neither sees Him nor knows Him; but you know Him, for He dwells with you and will be in you. I will not leave you orphans; I will come to you"
-John 14: 15-18.

I remember on one occasion, I came back from evangelism just to find out that we were about to write a test in Economics. It was during my fourth year in the High School. I prayed in the Holy Spirit (in unknown tongues 1Corinthians 14:14), asking the

Lord to help me. As I was still standing outside, my eyes suddenly went straight to a copy of Key Point and a little voice in my heart told me to pick it up. A Key Point is a little book with the summary of certain definitions in a certain subject. The book was lying on the floor.

It was as if someone had kept it there for me, perhaps one of my classmates left it there, but the Lord used it. By the time I picked it up, everyone was already seated for the test and the teacher was about writing on the chalkboard. Then the Lord showed me where to read, just in two pages, which I did. By the time I rushed into the class, I was surprised that the questions did not exceed what I had read from those two pages.

I later became so close to my Economics teacher and he offered to publish one of my tracts free of charge. It always pays to pray because God answers prayers. To me, it keeps me closer to the Father.

I do not believe that many souls would have come to the Lord through those my early efforts without intercessory prayers and God's Holy Spirit whom I got acquainted with from the age of five. I have found Him to be a true Comforter in my moments of tears and unpleasant experiences. He is that special Someone to talk to when no one else would understand me.

The Holy Spirit has been my precious and intimate Friend, my patient Teacher, my never failing Strengthener and my heartfelt Comforter in the darkest and loneliest moments of my life.

He brought me up in the supernatural and taught me how to love, to worship, and to be joyful and pray even in pain.

I have known Him as a great burden bearer and a trustworthy Confidant, through practical life experiences. And, I enjoy the benefit of the faithful promise of our Lord which says, I will not live you comfortless as orphans but I will come to you (John 14:18). I can boldly say with unwavering assurance that Jesus has made that promise good; He has come to us in His Spirit.

The Holy Spirit is God the invisible!

OUR HELPER IN PRAYER

The Holy Spirit helps us to pray when we are willing to pray. Yet, even when we feel too weak, He is strong in us and for us. I've woken up from sleep many times and caught my spirit still praying in the Spirit, in unknown tongues. When the body is asleep, the spirit is awake and quickened by the Holy Spirit. True intimacy with the Spirit will bring us to where our life will always glorify Christ, even in our sleep.

The Spirit will teach us from the Word, how to advance the Kingdom of God through intercessory prayers if we would yield to Him, engage His wisdom and follow the inward witness of His gentle voice. The Word of God is the wisdom of God (Luke 11:49).

The Holy Spirit is the Spirit of grace and the message and knowledge of grace releases Him to freely flow. It is neither by power nor by might that we will be able to prevail in the race of life and fulfil the tasks assigned to us but by the Spirit of the Lord. If we are grace-minded, we will be love-minded and Spirit-filled. But, if we are law-minded, we will be resisting the Spirit. For God Who ministers to us the Spirit, and works miracles among us does not do so by the works of the law but by the hearing of faith which is of grace (Galatians 3:5). We must understand and proclaim the message and shout of "grace, grace, grace!" If we will flow with the Spirit in these last days; *"So he answered and said to me: "This is the word of the LORD to Zerubbabel: 'Not by might nor by power, BUT BY MY SPIRIT,' SAYS THE LORD OF HOSTS. 'Who are you, O great mountain? Before Zerubbabel you shall become a plain! And he shall bring forth the capstone With shouts of "GRACE, GRACE TO IT!"''* (Zechariah 4:6-7).

We must grow fast in the knowledge of Christ. God asks us to consider the end of the conversation of those who have joined the cloud of witnesses. That means to start from where they have stopped. So, greater than all that has ever been done by people is still yet to be done, for the best wine is kept for the last generations (Hebrews 13:7-8).

Whatever God has done through people in the past, He wants to do the same and even greater today. He has not changed but many of us have really grown cold and weary. God has so much more in reserve for us today than we can ever ask or imagine.

CHAPTER 6

HOW TO RECEIVE A PROPHET'S REWARD

"Whoever receives you receives me, and whoever receives me receives Him who sent me. Everyone who receives a prophet, because he is a prophet, will receive a prophet's reward, and everyone who receives a righteous man, because he is a righteous man, will receive a righteous man's reward"
-Mathew 10:40-41 (WNT).

I began preaching the gospel the morning after the Lord Jesus Christ first appeared to me in mama's little room at the age of five. That encounter transformed my life. It bonded my heart to compassion forever. You see, you can listen to a thousand sermons and forget. You can also read a thousand books and not remember. But if you see Jesus even for a split second, it will remain with you forever!

Over the years, I have observed that both the result and impart of my ministry has largely been determined by how the people received me. I have not been able to impart lives where I have been dishonoured or rejected. Just like Jesus couldn't really make impart where He was dishonoured or rejected; *"But in the next breath they were cutting Him down: "we've known Him since He was a kid; He's the carpenter's Son. We know His mother, Mary. We know His brothers James and Joseph, Simon and Judas. All His sisters live here. Who does He think He is?" They got their noses all out of joint. But Jesus said, "A prophet is taken for granted in his hometown and his family." He didn't do many miracles there because of their hostile indifference"* (Mathew 13:55-58 MSG).

THE LAW OF HONOUR

Honour is a spiritual law. Once it is violated, you're disqualified for spiritual blessings. Jesus said, *"You will not see me again until you say, blessed is He who comes in the name of the Lord"*. This doesn't only speak of His return but it also means that we will not see Him till we begin to honour, receive and to bless those who come in His name (Mathew 23:39).

God comes in His messengers but you must look pass their appearance and flaws to see Him in His fullness in them. The prophet you dishonour will not reward you. The anointing you despise will not impart you.

I remember giving a prophetic word that a certain woman was going to conceive. It was another woman who was just passing by and had been barren for 12 years that received the word. She held it preciously and conceived the following month.

People's faith always limits their height in spiritual accomplishment. Prophets are God's agents of deliverance and preservation; *"By a prophet the*

LORD brought Israel out of Egypt, And by a prophet he was preserved"* (Hosea 12:13).

Faith in God will get you established but you must receive and believe His prophets for that establishment to prosper. Prophets are God's agents of prosperity; *"...Believe in the LORD your God, and you shall be established; BELIEVE HIS PROPHETS, AND YOU SHALL PROSPER"* (2Chronicles 20:20). Failure to receive those the Lord has sent to them is why some people are still meddling with poverty and frustration today.

Jesus said that blessed are those who are not offended because of Him (Mathew 11:6; Luke 7:23). If you let the devil deceive you into getting offended at the prophet that God has sent to bless you, he will cheat you out of your blessing.

God's prophets are sustained by divine supply. So, when God brings you the opportunity to meet their need, it is because He wants to meet your needs. The widow of Zarephath would have missed out on God's blessing supposing she refused the prophet's request. God was feeding the prophet by supernatural means. He was drinking from the brook of Cherith and the ravens were feeding him regularly. But when the brook dried, instead of God to give Him another source of water, He sent him to Zarephath because He didn't want a poor widow to die of starvation.

Don't ever think that you're helping the prophets that you're feeding. Instead, see it as a great priviledge because God is looking at your heart.

You see, sometimes, God can make His prophet hungry just because He wants to bless someone who will feed him. God of mercy and great compassion could not give that widow a miracle supply until she first fed His prophet. He blesses by multiplication. The little you're holding back may be keeping you from God's plenty. You're only generous towards God to the degree to which you're generous towards His people. Giving will enlarge your life. It will bring you supernatural favour;

1KINGS 17:1-16
1 ¶ And Elijah the Tishbite, of the inhabitants of Gilead, said to Ahab, "As the LORD God of Israel lives, before whom I stand, there shall not be dew nor rain these years, except at my word."

2 Then the word of the LORD came to him, saying,
3 "Get away from here and turn eastward, and hide by the Brook Cherith, which flows into the Jordan.
4 "And it will be that you shall drink from the brook, and I have commanded the ravens to feed you there."
5 So he went and did according to the word of the LORD, for he went and stayed by the Brook Cherith, which flows into the Jordan.
6 The ravens brought him bread and meat in the morning, and bread and meat in the evening; and he drank from the brook.
7 And it happened after a while that the brook dried up, because there had been no rain in the land.
8 ¶ Then the word of the LORD came to him, saying,
9 "Arise, go to Zarephath, which belongs to Sidon, and dwell there. See, I have commanded a widow there to provide for you."
10 So he arose and went to Zarephath. And when he came to the gate of the city, indeed a widow was there gathering sticks. And he called to her and said, "Please bring me a little water in a cup, that I may drink."
11 And as she was going to get it, he called to her and said, "Please bring me a morsel of bread in your hand."
12 So she said, "As the LORD your God lives, I do not have bread, only a handful of flour in a bin, and a little oil in a jar; and see, I am gathering a couple of sticks

THE TRANSFERENCE OF SPIRITS

that I may go in and prepare it for myself and my son, that we may eat it, and die."
13 And Elijah said to her, "Do not fear; go and do as you have said, but make me a small cake from it first, and bring it to me; and afterward make some for yourself and your son.
14 "For thus says the LORD God of Israel: 'The bin of flour shall not be used up, nor shall the jar of oil run dry, until the day the LORD sends rain on the earth.'"
15 So she went away and did according to the word of Elijah; and she and he and her household ate for many days.
16 The bin of flour was not used up, nor did the jar of oil run dry, according to the word of the LORD which He spoke by Elijah.

You see, your attitude towards God's prophets will determine whether you receive or not. A certain woman of understanding who had no child was in the habit of constantly begging the prophet Elisha to eat in her house. In fact, she eventually persuaded her husband that they should make a room for him in their house.

Eventually, through prophetic declarations, she conceived. She maintained that relationship with the prophet so much that even when the enemy came and took that child, she was free to go to him and desire a miracle. The child lived again;

2 KINGS 4:8-37

8 ¶ Now it happened one day that Elisha went to Shunem, where there was a notable woman, and she persuaded him to eat some food. So it was, as often as he passed by, he would turn in there to eat some food.
9 And she said to her husband, "Look now, I know that this is a holy man of God, who passes by us regularly.
10 "Please, let us make a small upper room on the wall; and let us put a bed for him there, and a table and a chair and a lampstand; so it will be, whenever he comes to us, he can turn in there."
11 And it happened one day that he came there, and he turned in to the upper room and lay down there.
12 Then he said to Gehazi his servant, "Call this Shunammite woman." When he had called her, she stood before him.
13 And he said to him, "Say now to her, 'Look, you have been concerned for us with all this care. What can I do for you? Do you want me to speak on your behalf to the king or to the commander of the army?'" She answered, "I dwell among my own people."

THE TRANSFERENCE OF SPIRITS

14 So he said, "What then is to be done for her?" And Gehazi answered, "Actually, she has no son, and her husband is old."

15 So he said, "Call her." When he had called her, she stood in the doorway.

16 Then he said, "About this time next year you shall embrace a son." And she said, "No, my lord. Man of God, do not lie to your maidservant!"

17 But the woman conceived, and bore a son when the appointed time had come, of which Elisha had told her.

18 ¶ And the child grew. Now it happened one day that he went out to his father, to the reapers.

19 And he said to his father, "My head, my head!" So he said to a servant, "Carry him to his mother."

20 When he had taken him and brought him to his mother, he sat on her knees till noon, and then died.

21 And she went up and laid him on the bed of the man of God, shut the door upon him, and went out.

22 Then she called to her husband, and said, "Please send me one of the young men and one of the donkeys, that I may run to the man of God and come back."

23 So he said, "Why are you going to him today? It is neither the New Moon nor the Sabbath." And she said, "It is well."

24 Then she saddled a donkey, and said to her servant, "Drive, and go forward; do not slacken the pace for me unless I tell you."

25 And so she departed, and went to the man of God at Mount Carmel. So it was, when the man of God saw her afar off, that he said to his servant Gehazi, "Look, the Shunammite woman!.

26 "Please run now to meet her, and say to her, 'Is it well with you? Is it well with your husband? Is it well with the child?'" And she answered, "It is well."

27 Now when she came to the man of God at the hill, she caught him by the feet, but Gehazi came near to push her away. But the man of God said, "Let her alone; for her soul is in deep distress, and the LORD has hidden it from me, and has not told me."

28 So she said, "Did I ask a son of my lord? Did I not say, 'Do not deceive me'?"

29 Then he said to Gehazi, "Get yourself ready, and take my staff in your hand, and be on your way. If you meet anyone, do not greet him; and if anyone greets you, do not answer him; but lay my staff on the face of the child."

30 And the mother of the child said, "As the LORD lives, and as your soul lives, I will not leave you." So he arose and followed her.

31 Now Gehazi went on ahead of them, and laid the staff on the face of the child; but there was neither

voice nor hearing. Therefore he went back to meet him, and told him, saying, "The child has not awakened."
32 When Elisha came into the house, there was the child, lying dead on his bed.
33 He went in therefore, shut the door behind the two of them, and prayed to the LORD.
34 And he went up and lay on the child, and put his mouth on his mouth, his eyes on his eyes, and his hands on his hands; and he stretched himself out on the child, and the flesh of the child became warm.
35 He returned and walked back and forth in the house, and again went up and stretched himself out on him; then the child sneezed seven times, and the child opened his eyes.
36 And he called Gehazi and said, "Call this Shunammite woman." So he called her. And when she came in to him, he said, "Pick up your son."
37 So she went in, fell at his feet, and bowed to the ground; then she picked up her son and went out.

The same anointing that produces a testimony is necessary to sustain it. Some people disconnect out of ingratitude or rebellion from those that God has sent to them or appointed over them. And as such, they have nowhere else to turn to when the devil afflicts them.

PROPHETS DO NOT SEE OR KNOW EVERYTHING

One of the most interesting parts of the previous story is when the prophet said that the Lord hid the woman's problem from him. Who could have thought that such a great prophet as Elisha would not have discerned the death of the child that was born through his own prophecy? God is not Man and man is not God! *"Now when she came to the man of God at the hill, she caught him by the feet, but Gehazi came near to push her away. But the man of God said, "LET HER ALONE; FOR HER SOUL IS IN DEEP DISTRESS, AND THE LORD HAS HIDDEN IT FROM ME, AND HAS NOT TOLD ME"* (vs 27).

You see, prophets are not expected to see and know everything. They're not supposed to manufacture revelations when the Spirit of the Lord is not operating it in them. That will be carnal or demonic divination.

So, people should not feel disappointed when God decides to hide some things from his prophets. Even the great apostle Paul declares by the Holy Spirit that we know in part and prophesy in part (1Corinthians 13:9).

I remember a certain woman who decided to forget everything that God has used a particular prophet to do in her life. She just discarded his ministry because something happened to her that he didn't see beforehand. How funny and irrational people could be sometimes. Some folks think that men of God are omniscient or all-knowing but that would have made them God and they're not God.

One of the most painful incidents of my life was the sudden departure of my grandmother. She was 84. I never knew that she would not return back home the day she waved me goodbye and went off to attend a funeral at the village. She was very healthy and looked like someone who could have lived for forty more years. I wasn't ready to let her go. There were spiritual classes she was taking me through that we had not yet concluded.

We were so close but the Lord did not show me that He was calling her home at the time.

About a year after she died, the Lord visited me in a vision. It was during the early morning hours. I asked Him why He hid such a vital event from me. He looked into my eyes with so much love and said; "Deuteronomy 29:29". When I got back in the natural, I checked my Bible and it reads; *"The secret things belong to the LORD our God, but those things which are revealed belong to us and to our children forever, that we may do all the words of this law."*

All the secret things belong to the Lord, only the ones that are revealed are for us. He has the right to hold back some things in His own wisdom. God is good even in pain. We must not allow the enemy mess with our mind and cause us to lose trust in God. Satan is like a scorpion. You cannot stop this scorpion from stinging, but you can stop it from stinging you and others who are within your spiritual domain or sphere of authority.

An old adage says that, you can't stop a bird from flying over your head but you can stop it from pitching a nest therein. *"Give no place to the devil"* is a sacred warning from the holy Word (Ephesians 4:27).

TESTIMONIES OF FAITH

The Centurion honoured Jesus so much that he said He doesn't have to come to his house for his servant to be healed.

He understood authority and the power of spoken words so, he begged Jesus to just speak a word; *"The Centurion replied, "Lord, I do not deserve to have you come under my roof. But just say the word, and my servant will be healed. Then Jesus said to the Centurion, "go! It will be done just as you believed it would." And his servant was healed at that very hour"* (Mathew 8:8, 13 NIV).

A woman who was probably inspired by the Centurion's story said unto me, "Just say a word and my son will be healed" and I told her, "Be it unto you according to your faith" and it was so, his son was healed of tuberculosis. *"He sent His word, and healed them, and delivered them from their destructions"* (Psalm 107:20).

Another woman said, "I placed your picture that I got online upon my only daughter who was mentally ill and she said she saw a brilliant light shone from the picture and was healed of her mental situation".

A certain man said to me, "Man of God, I begged you to receive my offering the last time you were in our Church and in that same month, I made my first million profits".

There are countless testimonies resulting from people's faith in God's prophets. Faith connects you to the boundless possibilities of God. It makes all that is possible to God possible to you.

Faith places demand on the ability of God in His prophets. The woman with an issue of blood said *"If I could only touch the fringe of His garment, I shall be made whole"* and the same garment that many have thronged with no effect made her whole because she touched it with faith (Mark 5:25-29). Faith produces extraordinary results.

Not everyone who says "Amen" to a prophetic word is entitled to be changed by it but only those who from their heart receive the prophet. You cannot be blessed by the ministry that you reject. Unbelief disqualifies from God's blessings. God in His prophet is a world of possibilities. Therefore, his declarations are not the mere words or empty sayings of a mere man. They carry the anointing of the Holy Spirit to make anything happen for anyone anywhere, according to their faith. Your faith will determine your experience. Faith is the link to God's supernatural power!

THE LINGERING ANOINTING

The anointing upon lingers. The lingering anointing follows the prophet's words and everything that proceeds from him, even long after his physical death.

It lingered upon the aprons and handkerchiefs that had contact with Paul and brought healing and deliverance unto many (Acts 19:11-12).

It lingered upon Peter's shadow and healed countless. People were bringing their sick from far and wide, both within and outside Jerusalem to the open squares or broad places so that his shadow might fall on them when he walks by. All of them were healed and it was not once or twice, it was a regular thing;

ACTS 5:14-17 (CEV)
14 Many men and women started having faith in the Lord.
15 Then sick people were brought out to the road and placed on cots and mats. It was hoped that Peter would walk by, and his shadow would fall on them and heal them.
16 A lot of people living in the towns near Jerusalem brought those who were sick or troubled by evil spirits, and they were all healed.
17 The high priest and all the other Sadducees who were with him became jealous."

Imagine that there were cameras back then. That anointing would have linger upon the words, videos, images and voices of those ministers of God and bring liberation unto many. The lingering anointing is upon the prophet's books, tapes, shadow, pictures and voice. It is upon his clothes, handkerchiefs, shadows, footprints, fingerprints and whatever has contact with him. It even robs off on whatever he sits upon. I remember how a young lady who stepped on a demonic poison and had a swollen

THE TRANSFERENCE OF SPIRITS

in her leg got healed. Her healing took place when she accidentally stepped on my shoes that I left at their door while I was on a visitation to the parents several years back. She said that she felt a current move through her legs like electricity and she was healed.

Years after the prophet Elisha had died, his decaying bones still carried the lingering anointing of the Holy Spirit for miracles; *"Once while some Israelites were burying a man, suddenly they saw a band of raiders; so they threw the man's body into Elisha's tomb. When the body touched Elisha's bones, the man came to life and stood up on his feet"* (2 Kings 13:21 NIV). If a dead Old Testament prophet's bone could bring the dead back to life, how much more shall people be blessed through a living New Testament prophet! Countless people have received the baptism with the Holy Spirit and spoke in tongues just reading my book or write ups. Many others have been healed and lots and lots have been saved.

An elderly woman who has heard of my ministry just like the woman with an issue of blood heard of Jesus' healing ministry shared her testimony. She said that she told her children on her sick bed,

"Just bring that prophet's picture and place it upon me and I will be healed" and that was the end of her long time paralysis! Glory to God! Yet, there are still so many who throng me daily but are just there, not receiving anything because they're either ensnared in the web of familiarity or unbelief.

THE DANGEROUS WEB OF FAMILIARITY
"Even my own FAMILIAR FRIEND in whom I trusted, Who ate my bread, Has lifted up his heel against me"
-Psalm 41:9.

Familiarity breeds dishonour which is a major hindrance to receiving the prophet's reward. Remember Judas was Jesus' familiar friend and instead of getting transformed by His ministry, he ended up betraying Him.

Familiarity can make you betray the anointing that should uphold and impart you. It can make the prophet look too ordinary by making you blind to the God inside him and exposing you to all his humanity.

THE TRANSFERENCE OF SPIRITS

How much can you receive? You're only limited to receive as much as your faith can conceive. So, believe in the Lord your God to be established and believe also in His prophets to prosper (2 Chronicles 20:20). In whose name do you receive your prophet? Is it as a brother, teacher or as a prophet? Don't just receive him in any name but in the name by which God appointed and anointed him. In the name of a prophet! Believe his words are from the Lord as long as they agree with the Word and honour the calling and anointing upon him.

Sow into that anointing and lay hold of all that your faith can conceive.

The anointing you sow into, you will flow into. Humble yourself to receive.

The anointing doesn't flow upwards, it flows downwards and it will not follow those who divide the Church but those who unite it; *"Behold, how good and how pleasant it is For brethren to dwell together in unity! It is like the precious oil upon the head, Running down on the beard, The beard of Aaron, Running down on the edge of his garments"* (Psalm 133:1-2).

If you make yourself a prophet's equal in your mind, you will not partake of the grace upon his life. Elisha was not Elijah's colleague, he was his apprentice. Pride and arrogance can hinder us from getting the double portion. Natural age and physical achievements are irrelevant as far as the transference of spirits is concerned. If you want the anointing, you must first humble yourself. The way down is the way up.

The transference of spirit is not for Absaloms who will divide their fathers' kingdom or Gehazis who are only interested in the profits of the ministry. It is for loyal Elishas and Joshuas, who are willing to serve their master from their heart.

Joshua was Moses' loyal servant; *"And Joshua the son of Nun, the servant of Moses, [one] of his young men, answered and said, My lord Moses, forbid them"* (Numbers 11:28 KJV). No wonder he was full of the spirit of wisdom after Moses had laid hands upon him; *"Now Joshua the son of Nun was full of the spirit of wisdom, for Moses had laid his hands on him; so the children of Israel heeded him, and did as the LORD had commanded Moses"* (Deuteronomy 34:9).

THE TRANSFERENCE OF SPIRITS

God promised to be with him as He was with Moses, his spiritual father (Joshua 1:5).

The double portion is for loyal servants and not those who break away prematurely. Even the laying on of hands will not work on you if your heart is not right.

I have seen many who break away out of rebellion but those who really get the double portion are loyal sons and daughters in the faith. You're faced up with a prophet's reward!

Be it unto you as you have believed in the name of Jesus Christ!

SAMSON AJILORE

Epilogue

ARE YOU REALLY SAVED?

"If you declare with your mouth, "Jesus is Lord," and believe in your heart that God raised him from the dead, you will be saved. For it is with your heart that you believe and are justified, and it is with your mouth that you profess your faith and are saved. As Scripture says, "Anyone who believes in Him will never be put to shame"
-Romans 10:9-11 (NIV).

BUT I GO TO CHURCH

Going to Church doesn't mean that you automatically have eternal life. If you've not made a conscious decision for Christ, don't think your name is written in the Lamb's book of life just because you attend Church services. You could even be a preacher or Sunday school teacher and not be saved. Salvation isn't an accident or unconscious decision. It is not something that happens automatically. It is a free gift of God obtainable by faith (Ephesians 2:8). However, God doesn't just write your name in the book of life or regenerate your spirit without your permission. Just because you're present in Church or do ministry doesn't mean you're born again.

BUT I'M A PREACHER

One could be a Pope and be unsaved. Salvation isn't a title, it is a decision, a New Creation, a new birth (2Corinthians 5:17-21). It is a very personal thing. I cannot be saved for you. Your parents cannot be born again on your behalf, no matter how much they love you. Salvation isn't earned by doing the work of God. Neither does it come with the title of a pastor, bishop, apostle or any other.

The world is full of many who try to spread the Christ they do not really know.

Jesus is not a story, He is a living Personality that can be known and experienced personally today! If you do not have a personal relationship with Him, you're publicizing Him in vain.

SALVATION BY ASSUMPTION

Don't just assume to be saved. Faith is not a baseless assumption; it is an offshoot of God's Word. Faith is rooted in the Scriptures and there's no Bible basis for assuming to be saved.

Jesus revealed to us from the encounter He had with Nicodemus in John 3 that one could be a superior religious leader and still be unsaved.

Nicodemus must have assumed he was saved until that night with the Saviour Himself. Don't be a Nicodemus and if you've been one, submit to the Word of God today.

INHERITED SALVATION?

Many go to Church because they were born into Christianity. Nevertheless, salvation is not physical hereditary. It is not transferable by genetics or heredity from earthly parents to their children.

Your father could be a Bishop and you still go to hell. If you search your heart and you find out that you have no memory of ever making a personal decision for Christ, it is better you do so now. Once that witness of the Holy Spirit is not in your heart or spirit that you're God's child, your eternity is unsure (Romans 8:16). Don't risk missing heaven!

BIBLE WAY TO BE SAVED

Romans 10:9-10 explains how to be saved. It says that you can do so by faith in Christ and confession. Salvation is free, not because it is worthless but because it is priceless. Should God put a price on an offer that cost Him the life of His only Son, who can afford it? None can, but in His infinite love and mercy, He decided to give us freely (John 3:16-18).

Here's a prayer of salvation based on that Scripture: "Dear God, I confess with my mouth the Lord Jesus Christ and I believe in my heart that you raised Him from the dead, I am saved!"

AN ADVICE FOR THE NEWLY SAVED

If you have said the above prayer, congratulations! You're now a New Creation, your past is gone forever, you're a new person (2Corinthians 5:17). I will advise you to get a Bible and begin to study. A good place to start is the Gospel of John, read and practice what you read. Talk to God, He's your Father now, you're free to discourse with Him every time, in the name of Jesus (John 1:12-13). He loves you and has no memory of any of your sins anymore (Hebrews 8:12).

Talk to Him about anything and everything that troubles you. He is interested in all that concerns you. You can also talk to Him anywhere because He is in your heart and can hear your thoughts and most silent whispers. Your heavenly Father loves you and has given you His Holy Spirit to guide you in all areas of your life, through the Bible.

Also, get plugged into a good local Church around you and be really committed. Don't cultivate the habit of ignoring Church (Hebrews 10:25). It is those who are really planted in God's house that will flourish in His court; *"Those who are planted in the house of the LORD Shall flourish in the courts of our God"* (Psalms 92:13).

A good Church is the one that believes and practices the Bible. It is a place where the Holy Spirit is allowed to operate freely, where everything is done to glorify Christ. God has placed people in the Church to help you grow (Ephesians 4:11-16).

There's no perfect Church but there's one that is perfect for you, where you can grow and be made ready for the Lord's return. Be spiritually alert, watching for the Lord and spreading the gospel (See Luke 12:35-40).

About the Author

Samson Ajilore is a strong apostolic voice and anointed prophetic teacher, theologian, pastor and author of over twenty-five life changing books. Sam is a living proof of God's grace and divine destiny. He's a son of prophecy, separated unto the Lord from the womb as His messenger of divine love to the nations (Jeremiah 1:5).

Sam teaches, prophesies and brings divine healing to the nations in partnership with the Holy Spirit. He came from a long line of apostolic and prophetic ministers and has been in the ministry since the age of five, following a divine encounter with the Lord Jesus Christ Himself. He's president at SAWO and Senior Pastor at Agapē Church of the Supernatural (ACOS).

Sam holds a Degree in Theology from the U.M.C.A. Theological College, Ilorin Kwara State, Nigeria. He's happily married to Fidelia and they are blessed with a son, Samson Oluwanifemi Ajilore. They live in Abuja, the Federal Capital Territory of Nigeria.

Please contact the author through the following address:

NIGERIA:
Samson Ajilore World Outreach
(SAWO),
P. O. Box 957 Kubwa,
FCT, Abuja Nigeria W/Africa
Email: agapevoice@live.com
Call: 08067419389.

USA:
Samson Ajilore World Outreach
(SAWO) International,
435, Fawcett Ave
#213 Tacoma, WA 98402
Email: sawousa@live.com
Call: +1 (253) 273-7933.

JOIN THE AGAPE PARTNERS

Dear friend, thank you for taking your time to read this message. I believe it has blessed you and it is my pleasure to extend to you the invitation to join the Agape Love Partners of SAWO today, so that we can both get this message to bless others around the world through our collective efforts.

You will become one with a large family of growing visionary people worldwide who are radical and desperate to get the Agape gospel of our Lord Jesus Christ across the globe with their sacrificial love and gifts.

Let us partner together in love and get this message out to others across the world. *"He who reaps receives wages, and gathers fruit to eternal life; that both he who sows and he who reaps may rejoice together"* John 4:36 (WEB).

If you have been blessed by this book, I will like to hear personally from you and lift you up to God in prayers.

To find out more about other books by Samson Ajilore:

Visit www.lulu.com/spotlight/agapevoice

Join Samson Ajilore on Facebook:

http://www.facebook.com/samson.ajilore

You can also follow Samson Ajilore on Twitter: @agapespirit

INTRODUCING THE WRITING MINISTRY OF SAMSON AJILORE

"...But His Word was in my heart like a burning fire shut up in my bones; I was weary of holding it back, And I could not"
-Jeremiah 20:9.

"What you see, write in a book and send it..." Revelation 1:11 *"Declare you among the nations and publish, and set up a standard; publish, and don't conceal..."*
-Jeremiah 50:2.

God sent Samson Ajilore as an apostolic voice with a definite mandate to liberate humanity from darkness into light through anointed words and to make God's unconditional love come alive in the consciousness of people of every tongue. Sam publishes the will of God to the body of Christ and the world at large. He is committed to spreading the gospel of Christ with love and power.

Sam's pen and passion has produced several anointed classics which are divided into several series. This includes such as the WOMEN LIBERATION SERIES (WLS) which consists of "Mercy

Said No!" and "The Chronicles of the Womankind" plus many more to come. Other series are the PROPHETIC ACTIVATION SERIES (PAS) which includes such anointed classics as "Becoming a Healing Prophet", "The School of the Seers", "Activating and developing the Prophet in You", "Maturing in the prophetic" and many more others. Then there are the SPIRITUAL GROWTH SERIES (SGS) which includes such classics as "Agape Love, what it really means", "The Agape Species", "The power of Unknown Tongues", and "A Course in Righteousness" among others.

Sam also has a SPECIAL EVANGELISM SERIES (SES) which includes the all-time evangelism classic "The Soul Winners" among others" The Soul Winners is among the free book projects which the friends and covenant partners of SAWO supports to make free mass distribution possible worldwide.

THE SAWO SERIES SEMINARS (SSS)

Each of the above series has their own seminar, where people are gathered and educated in the revelations discussed in those books. It is usually a place to meet with the author and be immensely blessed. Our seminars could be organized by our own ministry team or any serious minded and spiritually oriented ministry that invites us. We hold convergences across the nations where people are trained in the truth that sets them free. SAWO believes in the supernatural, not just in letters but in the demonstration of the power of the Holy Spirit resulting in miracles of healings, signs and wonders! *"And my speech and my preaching were not with persuasive words of human wisdom, but in demonstration of the Spirit and of power, that your faith should not be in the wisdom of men but in the power of God"* (1Corinthians 2:4-5).

THE WOMEN LIBERATION SEMINARS (WLS)

Women across the world have been subjected to all kinds of unpleasant experiences. Several suffer from gender discrimination, inferiority complex, insecurity, sex trafficking, bad marriages, domestic violence, illiteracy and other related issues. SAWO believes that God's World does not discriminate genders and that both women and men have equal worth and opportunity to be successful in life. It is true that the first woman was made from a man but thereafter every other human passed through a woman's womb. Women are now the cradle of humanity and their heads must not be bowed in shame but raised in grace and glory. SAWO attempts to restore women back to God's original intention by the power of the Holy Spirit and the Word of God in the WLS.

1. A Woman's purpose must be revealed as originally intended by the Creator.
2. Women must understand their prophetic destiny in the calendar of God
3. Women must understand the ongoing battle for their souls between light and darkness.
4. Women's sense of self-worth must be restored.
5. Their right to have and to determine choices must be restored.
6. They must have equal opportunities to resources as men.
7. Women must have the power to control their own lives as guided by God's Word.
8. The society must not deprive them of their rights anymore and women must learn to trust in God and release the creativity in their hearts for both national and international transformation.

INTRODUCING THE AGAPE VOICE OF THE SUPERNATURAL MEDIA

The Agape Voice of the Supernatural is the media ministry of Samson Ajilore World Outreach (SAWO) and it is dedicated to airing God's unconditional love in Jesus Christ, through the print media. *"For the earth shall be filled with the knowledge of the glory of the LORD, as the waters cover the sea"* - Habakkuk 2:14.

There is an ongoing media battle between light and darkness. If the Church does not take hold of the media to flood the earth with the knowledge of the glory God as the waters cover the sea (Habakkuk 2:14) then, we are failing in our duty. And, the devil will use the media to empower his own army against us by taking the minds of people and turning them into his own image, most especially our youths and the children. People must know the glory of the Lord as revealed in His love through Christ to be freed from the clutches of darkness that proceeds from the system of this world. We desire to raise an army of Agape love who will walk in the fullness of the Kingdom of God and conquer through love. The problem of the humankind started when their progenitors (Adam and Eve) ran away from love in the Garden of Eden but Love is running back unto us in Jesus Christ. It is time for us to embrace Him and to stay forever this time!

AVOS is for the sole purpose of airing the truth of God's love in Christ to people everywhere, beginning from Nigeria, Africa and to the rest of the parts of the world. Since people will be transformed into the image of that which they constantly behold, be it good or evil, we want to ensure that we fill every possible place with the Image of Christ, which is the Word of God so that people will begin to bear that Image (Romans 12:2; 2 Corinthians 3:18).

We believe that Christ in the Church is the hope of any nation and not its government because, although a government can influence peoples' minds through several measures of discipline and natural education, only God can change their hearts. The government can imprison criminals but only Christ can transform them into saints. There cannot be peace in a nation without Christ in the nation because He is the Prince of peace. As global shaking and religious terrors increases, the light of God must shine from the Church because when gross darkness grips the earth, it is a great opportunity for the glorious light to shine transcendently. Light belongs in the dark!

GOD IS SAYING UNTO HIS CHURCH:
"Arise, shine; for thy light is come, and the glory of the LORD is risen upon thee. For, behold, the darkness shall cover the earth, and gross darkness: but the LORD shall arise upon thee, and His glory shall be seen upon thee. And the Gentiles shall come to thy light, and kings to the brightness of thy rising" (Isaiah 60:1-3).

INTRODUCING THREE LIFE CHANGING CLASSICS BY SAMSON AJILORE

1. THE SOUL WINNERS

In this book the author releases a prophetic outcry for effective evangelism. He challenges believers from the Church walls out into the streets where sinners are. The author maintains that the Church is neglecting her primary assignment which is evangelism and calls the Church back into the Saviour's outcry which is to win souls. The great commission is all about soul winning and that is what "The Soul Winners" is all about. The reader will be taken on a journey of Christianity from the first century till date and the change between the first century Christian and the ones of nowadays are revealed. Every believer is called to be a soul winner and that is revealed in this book. The heartbeat of God is soul winning and that is the emphases in this book! You will see the divine circle of soul winning which was drawn from Romans ten and how every believer is in the last stage-called to witness!

2. THE POWER OF UNKNOWN TONGUES

The subject of tongues has been one of the most controversial topics in the body of Christ over the years. Some believe that it ended on the day of Pentecost but others argue that it continues today. Some believe that it is a gift for a selected few while others argue that it is for all. Many questions pop up on peoples mind when it comes to tongues:

1. Is tongue for today?
2. What exactly does tongue sound like?
3. Are tongues the evidence of the baptism with the Holy Spirit.
4. Can people be born again without speaking in tongues?
5. Will non tongue talking believers make it to heaven?
6. Why should anyone even speak in un-known tongues when God has given us understandable languages?
7. Why isn't tongue understood by people?
8. Who can speak in tongues?
9. Shouldn't tongues always be interpreted?
10. How does one know the genuine from the counterfeit?

11. How can one receive the baptism with the Holy Spirit and speak in tongues?
12. Which gift is the most important?
13. What is the difference between speaking in tongues and the gift of diversities of tongues?
14. What did Jesus and the apostles teach on tongues?

All these and many more questions are attempted biblically in this book. You will find out what happens when people get filled with the Holy Spirit and start speaking in tongues. The author draws from years of rich biblical experience on this subject. This book is a biblical attempt to address this subject in a way that will bring the reader to the understanding of it. It is both from the Bible and from close to a couple of decades experience on the baptism with the Holy Spirit and speaking in tongues. The author has experienced countless received the baptism and gifts of the Holy Spirit under his ministry and he is willing to share with you why and how to get this blessings!

This book will clear your doubts and answer your questions. It would inspire you and practically show you the way into this blessing of the Holy Spirit.

You would come out of it with an experience with God that you will never forget. You too will be filled with the Holy Spirit and magnify God in new tongues!

3. ACTIVATING AND DEVELOPING THE PROPHET IN YOU

This practical book provides insights on how to:
- Develop your prophetic gifting
- Move more strongly in the anointing
- Pray more effectively
- Know where you belong
- Intercede for your loved ones
- Understand divine direction in life and ministry

There's no how we can really discuss the prophetic without mentioning intercession. The first person to be addressed as a prophet in the Bible was an intercessor. His name is Abraham (Genesis 20:7). In fact, he was to pray for a man who had unknowingly snatched his wife. We do not really see Abraham going about and prophesying over everyone but we do see him standing in gap for nations. He pleaded with God over the rebellious cities of Sodom and Gomorrah.

Prophets are God's intimate friends with whom He shares His heart so that they can intercede.

God doesn't give us revelations about people and nations to boost our fame or increase our ego. I have observed that when people become intercessors, they begin to see. God wants praying people. Not those who will only pray for their own concerns. He wants those who can take hold with Him and intercede for the birthing of His purpose and plan upon earth. The cry in God's heart is the maturity of His Church. Baby Christians do not care about other people. They only want others to care for them. They bear no one's burden but they're burdens for everyone. The prophetic is deepened through a culture of intercession. If we really want to know and see, we must be ready to pray for others. Everyone has desires but maturity is when we can put our desires aside and seek the burden of the Lord's heart. God's burden is discernible in intercession.

Intercession is a profitable training ground for the prophetic ministry and it is where prophetic experiences increase. God always want to share His secrets with His family and He wants to give us directions in intercessory prayers. Sometimes, the message of guidance, or a word from the Lord that is necessary for us at the moment, will just come as a thought or an impression upon our mind. All these and many more are the prophetic experiences that are increased through prayers. When we intercede, we improve our spiritual sensitivity and purify our prophetic visions.

SAMSON AJILORE